BRAD BONDHUS

HISTORY UNCOVERED
Revealing Hidden Truths

SILVERSMITH
PRESS

Published by Silversmith Press—Houston, Texas
www.silversmithpress.com

ISBN 978-1-961093-62-1 (Softcover Book)
ISBN 978-1-961093-63-8 (eBook)

This book is dedicated to my wife of 42 years Debbie.
Also, my children Megan and John,
my daughter-in-law Stephanie
and grand-daughter Margo.

CONTENTS

ACKNOWLEDGMENTS

As a first-time author I was blessed with great reviewers who helped me find my writing legs. Brian gave a virtual slap on the side of the head challenging me to temper my writing style. In addition, his historical Insite, helped better focus my own historical perspective. John shared important details regarding Baltimore city which added depth to the message. Dale and Don shared from their experiences and helped smooth out some rough edges.

I need to thank Joanna for the writer training sessions aimed at helping novices like myself become the writer I may one day be. And finally, to my editor Pat for guidance in the final phases.

INTRODUCTION

We've all heard news reports or a detail of history and said, "That's interesting. I didn't know that." Likewise, we've all heard some news and been shocked or upset by the report. Have you ever heard a story and felt you were being lied to? I have. If so, you have the option of ignoring the story; just pay no attention to it. Or you can search for the truth so as not to be deceived.

My family bought a used car in July 2008. After agreeing on the price and value of the trade we sat down with the loan officer. After a prolonged absence the loan officer returned puzzled by his findings. His comment was that in spite of a very good credit score, the best interest rate we could get was 15 percent. He explained that just the day before the interest rates had been much lower. He had no explanation for the high rate. Something had changed overnight.

A few months before the US House of Representatives had been conducting hearings on the use of steroids in major league baseball. At the time I thought there must be something more important for Congress to work on. The hearings dragged on and resulted in Roger Clemons[1] being charged with lying to Congress.

By mid-September I suddenly found out why I was stuck with a high interest auto loan. The 2008 financial meltdown, known as the Great Recession, was getting into full swing. The Great Recession felt 'round the world! John McCain decisively suspended his presidential campaign to rush back to Washington, DC, to address the crisis. Barack Obama felt he could multitask. This was great political theater. With all the financial data available to the government I couldn't believe no one saw the storm brewing. I believe it's more likely everyone knew something was coming and wanted to distance themselves from any responsibility. In reality, both political parties had contributed to the problem with policies/legislation dating back decades.

So why was the House of Representatives looking into steroids in Major League Baseball? In my opinion Speaker of the House Nancy Pelosi and minority leader John Boehner did not want to take action to avoid a pending banking crisis for fear of being blamed for triggering the crisis during an election year. Therefore, Roger Clemons was a distraction to keep Congress, press, and public occupied for a while. All of Washington, DC, was getting ready to point fingers.

By this time my children were grown, and I had more time to reflect on life and what the media, government, and academia had told us over the years. I decided I needed

to get more involved to gain my own perspective on what was going on in the country. In 2009 I began volunteering with Habitat for Humanity in the Sandtown Winchester neighborhood of Baltimore. My first Habitat workday brought tears to my eyes as we turned off Route 40 onto Fulton Ave. That's when I saw firsthand the dilapidated buildings and despair which decades of politicians' promises had failed to correct. Later I began working with a nearby church. Riots occurred in this neighborhood in 2015 after the death of Freddie Gray during an arrest by Baltimore police.

I began to realize my education, the news, and what we were being told did not square with life experiences. Since then, I have been looking into history and believe we as a people are being manipulated to keep "We the People" divided. This text is my attempt to look at American history and explore these thoughts.

It's my contention that American government and its cultural institutions have been used to divide and pit the public against one another. By restricting the flow of information we've been collectively "gaslit" to accept a distorted understanding of our society. In so doing the forces controlling society maintain power.

The Merriam Webster Dictionary offers several definitions for gaslighting. The following best captures my intent:

"Gaslight: to grossly mislead or deceive (someone) especially for one's own advantage."[2]

My belief is that the "someone" in this definition is

We the People and the "one" is a group of elites that has been dividing, manipulating, and misinforming society for a century or more. The concept of gaslighting in politics was presented in Forbes Magazine where they stated: "It's not uncommon for a politician or political entity to use gaslighting as a tactic to divert public discourse and use manipulation to garner support for or against a certain viewpoint."[3]

In the 1999 box office hit The Matrix[4] one of its most iconic scenes is where our hero Neo is being invited on a journey that will radically alter and contradict everything he knows about life. He has a choice to make. The character Morpheus offers him two pills. A blue one or a red one. The blue pill will erase the fact that they ever met and any awareness Neo has about what is known of the matrix. With the blue pill Neo can go back to his ordinary life working in an ordinary cubicle and live the status quo like everyone else.

The red pill, however, is another story. The red pill will open his eyes to live fully in reality. It will allow him to see and understand the matrix which is keeping the human race unknowingly in a deep sleep and disillusionment. With the red pill he will wake up and get control of his life for the first time ever. And just before Neo chooses one of the pills Morpheus says:

Morpheus: "I imagine you feel a bit like Alice tumbling down the rabbit hole. You have a look of a man who accepts what he sees because he's expecting to wake up.

Ironically this is not far from the truth. Do you believe in fate Neo?

Neo responds: No.

Morpheus: Why not?

Neo: Because I don't like the idea that I'm not in control of my life.

Morpheus: I know exactly what you mean. Let me tell you why you're here.

You are here because you know something. What you know you can't explain but you can feel it. You felt it your entire life. That there is something wrong with the world. You don't know what it is but it's there. Like a splinter in your mind, driving you mad. It is this feeling that has brought you to me. Do you know what I'm talking about?

Neo: The Matrix.

Morpheus: Do you want to know what it is? The Matrix is everywhere, it is all around us. Even now in this very room. You can see it when you look out your window or when you turn on your television. You can feel it when you go to work, when you go to church, when you pay your taxes.

It's the world that has been pulled over your eyes to blind you from the truth.

Neo: What truth?

Morpheus: That you are a slave Neo. Like everyone else you were born into bondage, born into a prison that you cannot smell, or taste, or touch. A prison for your mind. Unfortunately, no one can be told what the Matrix is. You have to see it yourself. This is your last chance, after this there is no turning back. You take the blue pill and the story ends. You wake up in your bed and believe whatever you want to believe. You take the red pill and you stay in wonderland and I'll show you how deep the rabbit hole goes. Remember, all I'm offering is the truth nothing more.[5]

When historians write about history, they are assembling a puzzle with some of the pieces missing. The historian picks the heroes and villains, those we'll cheer or jeer in the future. They should include the details important to a thorough understanding without mundane superfluous details. But suppose they leave out important details which if included would shed negative light on their cause; details that may change the understanding of a situation significantly and therefore deceive. Sadly, these details may be lost to history unless discovered at a later date.

During my journey I realized my understanding of our country, the United States of America, was far from complete. I felt as though I needed to unplug from the academia, media, and government matrix to broaden my perspective to arrive at a deeper understanding of who we are as a nation. To sort through the divisions in our society we need to reflect on our experiences and what we've been taught with an open mind.

My trip down the rabbit hole began when I learned of shocking history regarding Woodrow Wilson which I expand upon later. In the chapter on Systemic Racism, I discuss an article from the Harvard Review which included a disturbing admission of past atrocities from the Progressive Era. Both facts have been hidden for decades if not generations.

In this book I attempt to shed light on a deceptive history perpetrated on *We the People*. It is not my intent to present a detailed account of American history but rather to fill in some pieces I feel important. Will you put this book down and take the blue pill? Or will you take the red pill and use this book to begin your own journey in search of the truth and cultural unity? In the 1970s Americans could have a spirited conversation over issues, agree to disagree but remain friendly. That is not the case today. It is by design and manipulation who writes history, who assembles that puzzle. Let's look at it now.

CHAPTER 1
THE RULING ELITE

I've heard it said, "History is written by the victors." This saying is not unique to our country. However, we speak of the American Revolution as a War for Independence while the British considered it a treasonous rebellion. During junior high history class, we learned of the Battle of the Little Bighorn (or Custer's Last Stand) as a massacre. During an interview years later Sitting Bull said:

> "These men who came with the Long Hair were as good men as ever fought...There were no cowards on either side. They fought. Many young men are missing from our lodges. But is there an American squaw who has her husband left? Were there any Americans left to tell the story of that day? No."[1]

For Sitting Bull, it was a great victory, one of the last for the plain's tribes.

I attended public schools during the civil rights movement of the 1960s. Our studies included the Progressive Era,

Teddy Roosevelt and his Rough Riders, his days in Montana, ascension to the Presidency and trust busting. TR wanted to make government work for the public not big corporations and monopolies. We learned of Woodrow Wilson, the creation of the Federal Reserve, the National Parks, prohibition, WWI, and the League of Nations. Academia must select what to teach. It's not possible to include every detail of every personality. Ultimately, my class was taught that the American people grew tired of progressive big government policies and selected a different path in 1920.

About 2006 I learned disturbing history regarding Woodrow Wilson which was not taught in my public-school history class; history not discussed in the media during the coverage of the 1960s civil rights movement. I will address this important puzzle piece later. It is this knowledge that sent me off on my journey down the rabbit hole.

Throughout the 1800s and early 1900s most American citizens did not attend college or university. In the early 1800s the economy was primarily agricultural, and most people lived a farm life with little time for formal education. That is not to say all people were ignorant, they did have books and candles or oil lamps and would read at night after the day's work was done. Abraham Lincoln was famously self-educated. The "Rail Splitter" would walk miles to borrow books. In addition, Abe apprenticed for his training as a lawyer. The prominent American universities remained in the east, the Ivy League.

So, who were the people that attended Ivy League universities and other institutions? Who was selecting the pieces for America's history puzzle? From the 1600s until the mid-1900s college graduates came predominantly from families with sufficient disposable income to send their sons away to study. In the vernacular of today, the privileged. Until the latter half of the 20th century Ivy League students were almost exclusively wealthy white males.[2] The wealthy of the north and south often shared family, social, business, financial, and educational ties. During the colonial and antebellum periods, the wealthy of the Carolinas and Georgia would vacation and conduct business in the north during the hot summer months. Likewise, the wealthy of the north would vacation in the south during the cold winter months. I learned this fact in local history museums in Newport Rhode Island and Charleston South Carolina. There was a trend among the wealthy to marry well. They wanted to make certain their daughters married men of means and their sons did not marry beneath their station.

A case in point Harvard graduate and future US President, Theodore Roosevelt Jr. had been upset that his father did not fight for the Union during the Civil War.[3, 4] Theodore Roosevelt Sr had married Martha Stewart Bulloch, whose father was James Stephens Bulloch of Georgia. Mr. Bulloch was a wealthy planter who owned over thirty slaves and a partnership in a cotton mill. Teddy's mother did not want her husband to fight against her family. Martha's brother Irvine served in the Confederate Navy on the CSS *Alabama*, then on the CSS *Shenandoah* as sailing master.[5, 6] The Civil War ended in 1865 but tremendous gaping wounds and turmoil remained. After all, this was the war where "brothers fought brothers and cousins fought cousins." The southern economy was devastated during the war. I would like to focus on those southern elites who came north to establish a fresh start in New York City. I happen to be a fan of historical mini-series; the most recent is *The Gilded Age* created by Julian Fellows on HBO Max. This series gives historical insight into glitz and glamor as well as snootiness of New York high society in the late 1800s and early 1900s. *The Gilded Age* introduced me to a remarkably interesting character, Ward McAllister.

Ward McAllister, originally from Savana Georgia, is chiefly remembered now as the inventor of the phrase, "the Four Hundred." Although purported to be an index of New York's best families, McAllister's list was suspiciously top-heavy with nouveau riche industrialists and McAllister's southern allies seeking a new start in the nation's financial capital after the American Civil War. With his smooth southern nature, McAllister served as Mrs. Astor's right-hand man.[7, 8, 9] His chief business and pleasure in life was to help Mrs. Astor guard the gates to New York High Society. Among the undesirables McAllister endeavored to exclude from the charmed circle of the Four Hundred were the many nouveau riche Midwesterners who poured into New York seeking social recognition.

Several southerners that moved north after the Civil War were prominent members of the United Daughters of the Confederacy. Included was Varina Davis, First Lady of the Confederacy as well her daughter. Varina Davis is purportedly a distant cousin of Kate Davis Pulitzer, wife of Joseph Pulitzer. Varina Davis wrote a regular column for Joseph Pulitzer's "New York World".[10, 11, 12] It's said she worked to reconcile prominent figures of the North and South.

Another was Sara Pryor, wife of Roger Pryor, a former confederate officer who studied law in New York City. The couple became prominent among several influential southerners in New York who were known as "Confederate carpetbaggers."[13]

SO, WHO WRITES HISTORY?

The majority of students attending American universities in the 1700 and 1800s was of a class of privileged elites from the wealthy in society, many of whom benefited from slavery either directly or indirectly. This was a class of elites who forgot about the contention within the founding generation over the issue of slavery. These elites forgot about the contradiction of demanding liberty for some while holding others in slavery. Many of these elites would return graduate and leave to pursue various business interests. However, those who remained in academia would become the new faculty or administrators.

The US economy grew rapidly after the American Civil War during America's second industrial revolution. Many great fortunes were made during this period as we progressed to the "Gilded Age" of the late 1800s, the Progressive Era (1890-1920). Regarding history, the professorial class were the guardians of history with an interpretation acceptable to the elite class. During the Progressive Era this country started moving toward a reliance on an "expert class" to manage our society. The business model of American universities included training the expert class that would run government.

About 2005 I watched a video that documented how Woodrow Wilson had resegregated the federal government. This documentary was on the history of the KKK and how the KKK was resurrected in 1915 during the Wilson Administration.[14]

Having grown up during the 1960s Civil Rights era, how was it I did not recall this important bit of history being discussed in school history class or on TV news? We were taught about the Klan after the Civil War. We also knew the Klan still existed in the south. We were not told the Klan had been ended during Reconstruction or that it was resurrected during the Progressive Era or that Woodrow Wilson had resegregated the federal government. Clearly, the powers that be did not want us to know these details.

I subsequently spoke with a neighbor, a black man some 20 years my senior. I knew he had participated in local civil rights protests in the '60s. When I mentioned this issue, this neighbor knew nothing of Woodrow Wilson's horrible history. When my neighbor later confirmed the history through another source, we were both surprised. This is when I began my journey down the rabbit hole.

CHAPTER 2
SLAVERY AND A NEW NATION

Southern Democrats claimed that slavery was a positive good to justify the institution. The claim was that the African slave was not able to govern his own life. They asserted they were too childlike in thought and that somehow a master could better guide them.

"As a good thing, slavery is strikingly peculiar, in this, that it is the only good thing which no man ever seeks for himself!" Abraham Lincoln, 16th President of the USA[1]

As previously mentioned, historians must choose what is important to include in a history text, therefore an individual or group of individuals decides what the narrative should be. Let me present my condensed recollection of many weeks of public-school classwork into a few paragraphs.

During my 8th or 9th grade history class in the upper Midwest, about 1968, we were taught that slavery existed in the colonies because numerous British kings declared it legal. There was a growing restlessness in the colonies. Many were looking for freedom from an oppressive English king. The colonies of Pennsylvania and Connecticut had passed laws banning slavery which King George disallowed. For some of this Revolutionary Generation, the issue of slavery was very repulsive, as slavery was inconsistent with the founding ideals. Subsequently the founding generation passed the Northwest Ordinance in 1787 which forbade slavery in the Northwest Territory. The states of Ohio, Michigan, Indiana, Illinois, and Wisconsin grew out of the Northwest Territory.

Our lessons stated that slavery as an institution was declining as the primary crops raised, rice, tobacco, indigo, and cotton were not very profitable. However, Eli Whitney's invention of the cotton gin reinvigorated the institution. Removal of the seeds from the cotton was very tedious by hand. The invention of the cotton gin accelerated the cleaning process making "King Cotton" the primary agricultural product of the south with slave labor used to grow, pick, and clean the cotton. As a result, exports of cotton to northern and European textile mills skyrocketed.

We learned of the blood spilled leading up to the Civil War. Pro and antislavery forces clashed in Bloody Kansas and Missouri. Steven Douglass, promoting the Missouri Compromise and Popular Sovereignty, brought the idea to let the folks in each new territory vote on the issue. There was regional tension over the Fugitive Slave Act, which was written to force northern citizens and abolitionists to return runaways or be punished. Southern Democrats started the Civil War by firing on Fort Sumter, followed by numerous battles, and the war ended with General Lee's

Surrender at Appomattox Court House. Finally, there was the assassination of the Republican President Abraham Lincoln by Southern Democrat John Wilkes Booth. I do not recall much of what we were taught regarding Reconstruction. There was the promise of forty acres and a mule and the naming of Carpetbaggers and Scalawags. Carpetbaggers were northerners who came south for financial gain, and to help educate and politically organize the freed slaves. Scalawags were southerners doing the same. That was followed by the Jim Crow South, and Southern Democrats.

History was not my favorite topic, I will admit. So, if there was more that I am overlooking I apologize. I do not remember the discussion of slavery in North America before European settlement, but it did exist. In fact, slavery has been part of the human condition for all of time. Past civilizations accepted slavery as a part of life. The ideal of individual freedom on which the USA was founded forced the founding generations to wrestle with the institution of slavery. Unfortunately, it took a Civil War to bring it to an end.

A conquering society generally considered slaves as part of the spoils of war. The Egyptian pyramids were built with slave labor as was the Great Wall of China and much of the Roman Empire. The Inca used slaves as human sacrifices to their gods. This book focuses on slavery on the North American continent.

NORTH AMERICAN SLAVERY BEFORE EUROPEAN COLONIZATION AND THE IMPACT OF THE AMERICAN REVOLUTION

The practice of slavery was not imported to the North American continent by Europeans. Native American tribes had their own practices of slavery. Many tribes practiced slavery taking captives from conquered tribes.

During a recent visit to Glacier National Park, we rode a tour bus driven by a member of the Black Foot Nation. The Park is a portion of the traditional Black Foot homeland. Our driver/guide mentioned that the Black Foot tribe are taller than surrounding tribes. Some of the surrounding tribes would kidnap Black Foot women for marrying and breeding purposes hoping their offspring would be taller.

Generally, tribal life in the southeast did not include commercial agriculture but subsistence farming. As a result, slaves were not members of a profit-driven enterprise. They worked alongside their masters performing daily chores. Masters could kill their slaves without retribution, but their enslavement was not hereditary. Slaves held by some Native American tribes could be adopted into a tribe, possibly as a replacement for a tribal member killed in war. In some instances, white slaves could marry into a tribe to gain their independence. Yes, white slaves; with conflict between colonists and tribes captured Europeans were often enslaved. Likewise, Europeans enslaved captured natives.[2] Often native tribes would ally with the French or British governments in conflicts between colonial powers or the British government against rebellious colonists. Colonial officials would reward Indian allies with African slaves and bounty for returned runaways.[3,4,5]

So how did the native tribes people treat Africans? The tribes had strict laws forbidding intermarriage between a native and an African slave. Punishment for natives who married an African was often banishment from the tribe. After the American Revolution and the Treaty of Paris in 1783, the tribes only had one white government to deal with, that of the new United States of America.

The elites of the tribes of the southeastern US believed they would need to adopt the culture of the elites of the southern whites. The elites of the "Five Civilized Tribes" attempted to integrate into the new social structure through intermarriage, education, and adoption of Christianity. The "Civilized Tribes" included the Cherokee, Chickasaw, Choctaw, Creek, and Seminole. Over several generations this trend toward "Americanization" among the elites included the development of plantation agriculture with large scale chattel slavery. Not all natives supported chattel slavery as there existed abolitionist movements within the tribes.[6]

THE DECLARATION OF INDEPENDENCE

On June 7, 1776, as instructed by the Virginia Convention, Richard Henry Lee, a relative of Robert E Lee, presented a resolution to the Continental Congress. The resolution stated: "that these United Colonies are, and of right ought to be, free and independent states." John Adams of Massachusetts seconded the motion and a debate raged for two full days. Finally, Congress tabled Lee's resolution for three weeks to allow delegates to receive feedback from their Colonial (soon-to-be-state) legislatures. A committee was appointed to work on a formal statement to be prepared should the resolution be accepted. The committee included John Adams, Roger Sherman of Connecticut, Robert R. Livingston of New York, Benjamin Franklin of Pennsylvania, and Virginia delegate Thomas Jefferson.

John Adams pressed Jefferson to take the lead writing for the following reasons: "Reason first, you (Jefferson) are a Virginian, and a Virginian ought to appear at the head of this business. Reason second, I (Adams) am obnoxious, suspected, and unpopular. You are very much otherwise. Reason third, you (Jefferson) can write ten times better than I can."[7]

Jefferson spent three weeks working on what became the Declaration of Independence. Much time was spent in consultation with the other committee members. Jefferson's first draft included the following charge against King George.

"He has waged cruel war against human nature itself, violating its most sacred rights of life and liberty in the persons of a distant people who never offended him, captivating and carrying them into slavery in another hemisphere or to incur miserable death in their transportation thither. This piratical warfare, the opprobrium of INFIDEL powers, is the warfare of the CHRISTIAN king of Great

Britain. Determined to keep open a market where MEN should be bought and sold, he has prostituted his negative for suppressing every legislative attempt to prohibit or to restrain this execrable commerce. And that this assemblage of horrors might want no fact of distinguished die, he is now exciting those very people to rise in arms among us, and to purchase that liberty of which he has deprived them, by murdering the people on whom he also obtruded them: thus paying off former crimes committed against the LIBERTIES of one people, with crimes which he urges them to commit against the LIVES of another."[8]

Before the Revolutionary War began King George had denied colonies the right to end slavery in a particular colony. His royal decree overrode the colonial legislatures. After the war began King George offered freedom to slaves that would abandon their masters and fight the Colonials.[9]

In his autobiography many years later Jefferson offered the following to explain why the clause was struck.

"The clause. . . reprobating the enslaving the inhabitants of Africa, was struck out in compliance to South Carolina and Georgia, who had never attempted to restrain the importation of slaves, and who on the contrary still wished to continue it. Our Northern brethren also I believe felt a little tender under these censures; for tho' their people have very few slaves themselves, yet they had been pretty considerable carriers of them to others." Thomas Jefferson[10]

At the signing of the Declaration of Independence Benjamin Franklin declared,

"We must all hang together, or most assuredly, we will all hang separately."[11]

They in fact were committing an act of treason in King George's eyes. A few of the signers were hunted down by British troops, their property confiscated, they were tortured and murdered for this action. Some colonists supported independence, others were loyal to the crown and a third group were neutral. Recent estimates are that roughly 40 percent supported independence, 20 percent supported the crown and the remaining roughly 40 percent were neutral.[12] Add to this division that members of the three groups were also divided by support for the continuances of slavery or abolition. This new nation had many serious divisions to resolve while attempting to maintain a stable social order during a war with the world's dominant superpower.

My public-school lessons regarding the "Founding Fathers" acknowledged that many were slaveholders and that some were conflicted. We did not discuss how the legal structure was established for this new nation. It had to be extremely difficult to establish a new legal system in the middle of a rebellion when some of your peers had already been murdered.

THE ESTABLISHMENT OF A NEW LEGAL SYSTEM
FOR VIRGINIA

Shortly after the Declaration of Independence was signed, the 13 original states adopted the "Articles of Confederation and Perpetual Union," defining the relationship between the states and federal government. Under these articles, the states remained sovereign and independent; Congress serving as the last resort on appeal of disputes. The Articles of Confederation named the new nation "The United States of America." Congress was given the authority to make treaties and alliances, maintain armed forces and coin money, nothing more. However, the federal government lacked authority to levy taxes and regulate commerce. The Articles were hastily written in 1777 due to urgency of war. However, progress in ratification was slow due to land claim disputes by states and fears of central authority.[13]

Given the fear of a strong central government, the bulk of the laws regulating society and commerce fell to each of the states individually. Each state began to evolve new laws from the form of British Common Law they were accustomed to as colonies. Colonial voting rights were defined by 18th century English notions regarding gender, race, financial success, and who had a personal stake. Typically, the vote was granted to a white, male property owner who was twenty-one years or older.[14]

The task of rewriting Virginia state laws was taken up by George Wythe, America's first professor of law, whose former students included Thomas Jefferson and Edmund

Pendleton.[15, 16] However, of the more than one hundred bills proposed to the legislature few were passed. During visit to Colonial Williamsburg, we had learned that Jefferson had attempted to change the institution of slavery to no avail. However, the concepts of religious freedom, public records, access to public education, and the concept of intermediate appellate courts became important concepts in the new republic.[17]

Each state began their own process to establish state laws beginning with the existing colonial laws. And so began the long struggle over slavery that many believed would lead to a civil war.

ENLIGHTENMENT INFLUENCE ON THE FOUNDING GENERATION

The American Revolution occurred at the height of the "Enlightenment" or "Age of Reason." Enlightenment thinkers, both secular and religious, questioned traditional authority. They thought humanity could be improved through rational change. Some of the Enlightenment thinkers in the colonies were Thomas Paine and Thomas Jefferson.[18]

During these revolutionary times, a spiritual revival was occurring in the UK as well as the colonies. John Wesley, the founder of the Methodist Church was attempting to reform the Church of England. John Wesley was an ardent abolitionist as he believed slavery was against God's Natural Law.[19, 20] The Presbyterian and Baptist Churches were other abolitionist influences at this time. Soon the invention of the cotton gin in 1793 made cleaning raw cotton much easier and the southern economy switched to "King Cotton." Southern wealth became concentrated in the large cotton plantations. The plantation owners dominated politics, state and national, the courts, and business. In addition, white southern clergy kept their church positions at the pleasure of the plantation owners.[21]

Modern critics chastise the Founding Fathers as hypocrites for promoting freedom while many themselves held slaves. Thomas Sowell points out that some who owned slaves detested the institution. We will discuss three Virginians for which this was the case. In each case these men inherited mortgaged estates of which the slaves were a part. By the laws of the day, the financial and legal obligations had to be settled before the slaves could be freed. In English society there was a strong tradition of stewardship of the family legacy. As such the family inheritance was not theirs to dispose of in their own lifetime but to pass on to the next generation as it had been passed on to them. Obviously, many slave owners considered their slaves a source of wealth and hence resisted emancipation.

George Washington was one of those who had inherited slaves. His will stated that his slaves would be freed, manumitted, on the death of his wife. George and Martha did not have any children together. His will also required that slaves too old and infirm to take care of themselves should be taken care of by his estate. He also required that the children be taught to read and write and train for a useful occupation. Washington's estate continued to pay for the support of some freed slaves for decades after his death as stipulated in his will. Washington's will stated, "I do hereby expressly forbid the sale of any slave I may die possessed of under any pretext whatsoever." Washington was searching for a plan as he wrote in a letter, "...to liberate a certain species of property which I possess very repugnantly to my own feelings".

George Washington was attempting to hold together a fragile coalition of states in rebellion against the world's dominant superpower. He could not afford to stir up contentious social issues that could not be resolved quickly.[22, 23]

Thomas Jefferson also inherited a mortgaged plantation. Jefferson saw the heavy moral stigma of slavery. He also recognized the social dangers to flesh and blood people, he wrote in a letter:

"I can say with conscious truth that there is not a man on Earth who would sacrifice more than I would to relieve us from this heavy reproach in any practicable way the possession of that kind of property for so it is misnamed is a Bagatelle which would not cost me a second thought if in that way a general emancipation and expatriation could be affected and gradually and with due sacrifices, I think it might be. But as it is we have the wolf by the ears, and we can neither hold him nor safely let him go. Justice is in one scale and self-preservation in the other."[24, 25]

Unfortunately, for numerous reasons Jefferson was greatly indebted at his death. His beloved Monticello, land, slaves, and most of his possessions were sold at auction. Jefferson's grandson, Thomas Jefferson Randolph eventually paid off the last of his grandfather's debts fifty years after Thomas Jefferson's death.[26]

The third Virginian is included because of an important connection to be made later. John Randolph, who never married, had inherited an estate along with existing debts. In his will Randolph wrote: "I give and bequeath all my slaves their freedom heartily regretting that I have ever been the owner of one. An earlier will said I give my slaves their freedom to which my conscience tells me they are justly entitled."[27, 28]

Thomas Sowell commented of Randolph: "That this was said by a conservative white Southerner a bitter political opponent of the abolitionists and a man who asserted the right of secession long before the civil war suggests something of the complexity of the issue."[29, 30]

As Thomas Sowell points out:

"[S]lavery was ubiquitous, existing all around the world. Furthermore, both secular and religious institutions of all major faiths accepted slavery as a normal part of life. In addition, the abolitionist movement in the Christian west was the impetus for ending slavery around the world. In fact, it was British imperialism that led to the suppression of slavery in British colonies around the world. As British abolitionist influence spread throughout Europe and North American slavery was eliminated in the Western Hemisphere."[31, 32]

These details regarding Washington, Jefferson, Randolph, and abolition of slavery in the Christian west are important pieces to add to the puzzle that is American history. It's important to note that founding a new nation demanded serious commitment of time and money by that founding generation. This commitment resulted in neglect of their responsibilities at home. George Washington was active in the Continental Congress before the Revolutionary War. General Washington was away from Mount Vernon for over eight years of the war. When Washington was President, the federal capital was in New York. Another 8 years away from Mount Vernon. Washington spent nearly seventeen of the last twenty-four years of his life away from Mount Vernon.[33]

After writing the Declaration of Independence Thomas Jefferson served in many capacities. Jefferson served in the Virginia legislature serving on the committee to rewrite colonial-state laws. He served as governor of Virginia then in the US Congress. From 1786 to 1789 Jefferson served as minister to France. Jefferson served as the first US Secretary of State from 1790 to 1793 under President Washington. He was the second Vice President under John Adams. Finally, Jefferson was President from 1801 to 1809. In total Jefferson spent over thirty years away from Monticello.[34]

I'm confident that others of the founding generation like Washington and Jefferson gave much in service to the nation yet ended up poorer as a result. For more background I recommend you watch the referenced YouTube video library titled,The End Of Slavery Explained - Full Compilation (youtube.com)[35]

WHAT WERE YOU THINKING MRS. VOBE?

Following is a separate case from the Colonial Era I thought worth including. During a visit to Colonial Williamsburg, I heard the story of Gowan Pamphlet, an enslaved person who preached to fellow enslaved persons. His mistress, Jane Vobe of the Kings Arms Tavern, manumitted all her slaves except Gowan Pamphlet. By law, an African, free or slave, was not allowed to preach. However, as an enslaved person whom Mrs. Vobe allowed to preach, he was protected as her property. At Mrs. Vobe's permission, Pamphlet was ordained in 1772 and became the only ordained black preacher of any denomination in the country. Inspired by the Great Awakening, Pamphlet preached a message of equality before God during the Revolution. He followed his calling to build Williamsburg's First Baptist Church, which continues to this day. But the risks were heavy. Large gatherings of African Americans were prohibited out of fear of slave uprisings and Baptist preachers faced harassment as dissenters from the officially recognized Church of England, even after Virginia's Statute for Religious Freedom ended state sponsorship of the church in 1786.[36]

3/5ᵀᴴ CLAUSE OF THE US CONSTITUTION

"Representatives and direct Taxes shall be apportioned among the several States which may be included within this Union, according to their respective Numbers, which shall be determined by adding to the whole Number of free Persons, including those bound to Service for a Term of Years, and excluding Indians not taxed, three fifths of all other Persons."[37]

The extremely weak and ineffective federal government resulting from the Article of Confederation led to the Constitutional Convention in 1787 for the creation of new federal laws under The United States Constitution.[38]

During the constitutional convention, some states insisted on counting their slaves as human beings for the purpose of representation in the House of Representatives. At the same time, they would not allow those same persons the right to vote, as they considered their slaves to be property.

Slavery existed in all states at the time of the revolution. Not because people voted on it but because King George would not allow any colony to abolish slavery. The northern colonies/states began to abolish slavery shortly after the Declaration of Independence. The southern colonies/states collaborated with northern sympathizers to maintain and expand slavery. The 3/5th clause was a bitter compromise to move forward with the constitution.[39] One can wonder if the Constitution would not have been realized at all if the abolitionist-leaning elements hadn't accepted this compromise. The infant country was barely holding together under the Articles of Confederation, and many compromises were made to get agreement on the Constitution.

Frederick Douglass shared the following interpretation of the 3/5th clause in 1860.

"It is a downright disability laid upon the slaveholding States; one which deprives those States of two-fifths of their natural basis of representation. A black man in a free State is worth just two-fifths more than a black man in a slave State, as a basis of political power under the Constitution. Therefore, instead of encouraging slavery, the Constitution encourages freedom by giving an increase of 'two-fifths' of political power to free over slave States." Frederick Douglass[40]

Douglass recognized that the three-fifths clause was written for the sole purpose of limiting congressional representation of the slave states and denied the slave states additional pro-slavery seats in the US House of Representatives. I had learned this revelation of Frederick Douglass in the 1960s. Douglass was not alone in this conclusion. Frederick Douglass also stated,

"Now, take the Constitution according to its plain reading and I defy the presentation of a single pro-slavery clause in it. On the other hand, it will be found to contain principles and purposes entirely hostile to the existence of slavery."[41]

How is it that a truth recognized by one of our chief abolitionists 160 years ago could be misconstrued today? The framers of the constitution were attempting to diffuse sectional tensions over slavery to maintain the union.[42] Modern day critics of the framers have flipped this argument on its head for the purpose of modern politics. One critic states, "Northerners might have stood their ground on liberty, and insisted on a stronger union, without counting slavery for representation..."[43]

To do so is an unfair castigation of delegates trying to create entirely new form of government, a government of self-rule with no monarch, king, emperor, or dictator. It's easy to cast stones two centuries after the fact. However, this modern position would have led to the immediate dissolution of the union they were desperately attempting to save.

THE NORTHWEST ORDINANCES

British General Cornwallis surrendered at Georgetown on October 19, 1781. The newly free nation was struggling to establish an American form of self-government. Having just broken free of the oppressive British Monarchy the patriots were averse to a strong central government; hence the federal government had little money or resources with which to operate.

CHAPTER 2: SLAVERY AND A NEW NATION

Several states ceded portions of the state to the federal government. These lands had been granted to the colonies by the British Monarchy during colonial times. Congress enacted a series of three ordinances (1784, 1785 and 1787) to define how these lands were to be developed, and how new territories and states were to be established and raise money for the bankrupt federal government. These ordinances put the world on notice, particularly Great Britain, that the newly formed United States of America was going to expand. The lands in question were north and west of the Ohio River and east of the Mississippi river, The Northwest Territory.

The Northwest Ordinance of 1787 was the most significant. Three principal provisions were defined in the document:[44]

1. A division of the Northwest Territory into "not less than three nor more than five States"

2. A three-stage method for admitting a new state to the Union: a congressionally appointed governor, secretary, and three judges to rule in the first phase; an elected assembly and one non-voting delegate to Congress to be elected in the second phase when the population of the territory reached "five thousand free male inhabitants of full age"; and a state constitution to be drafted and membership to the Union to be requested in the third phase when the population reached 60,000

3. A bill of rights protecting religious freedom, the right to a writ of habeas corpus, the benefit of trial

by jury, and other individual rights; in addition, the ordinance encouraged education and forbade slavery.

Though divided on the slavery issue, the Founding Fathers agreed that these lands, the Northwest Territory, would be free. Some likely agreed reluctantly, but they ultimately agreed. Or at least so it seemed. As previously mentioned, the invention of the cotton gin made cleaning the cotton much more viable economically. The greed of the planters hardened their hearts, they turned hard against freedom as they could profit from slave labor growing and picking cotton.

Unfortunately, slavery began to creep into the Northwest Territory. Southerners migrating into that region took their slaves with them under the guise of indentured servitude, which was legal in the territory. Most northerners who favored "free states" in which slavery was prohibited feared that slavery would become de facto in the states carved from the Northwest Territory.[45]

MISSOURI COMPROMISE

As the nation expanded, tension over the slave issue remained. There was a concerted effort to ensure a balance of slave vs free state in the US Senate. By the time Missouri applied for statehood in 1819, the north was concerned about admitting a new slave state. Fortunately, the more populous north had a slight advantage in the House of Representatives despite the 3/5th clause of the constitution.

New York Representative James Tallmadge, Jr. proposed the following two amendments to the Missouri statehood bill:[46]

1. The first outlawed "the further introduction of slavery or involuntary servitude" into Missouri.
2. The other created a timetable for gradual emancipation that freed every enslaved person born in the territory at the age of 25.

The House passed his amendments, along strictly regional voting lines, but the Senate rejected it.[47] Three days later, Tallmadge addressed the House of representatives with a defiant speech in which he argued that the Constitution empowered Congress to stop the expansion of slavery. For Tallmadge this was a long-held belief, twenty years earlier, in 1798, he gave a similar speech at his college graduation.

Tallmadge ended calling for universal emancipation.

"Then wish willingness present slaves be permitted to enjoy the sacred rights of fellow. Then will they have a country to love and defend, and when danger threatens then group with all true Yanks strong united with their Adams in their cabanet [sic] and their Washington in the field clasping the standards of liberty will swear to dwell free & independent or glory expire are inherent ruins."[48]

The fight over slavery continued until the district of Maine was divided from Massachusetts and sought statehood. The Speaker of the House, Henry Clay of Kentucky, proposed that Maine be admitted as a free state, and Missouri admitted as a slave state. Thus, the idea that states be admitted in pairs, one free and one slave was born. Illinois Senator Jesse B. Thomas proposed that slavery be allowed below the parallel, 36 degrees, 30 minutes the southern border of Missouri.[49] Finally, the Missouri Compromise was passed by the Senate on March 2, 1820, and the House on February 26, 1821.

FOUNDING OF THE DEMOCRAT PARTY

During the presidential election of 1824, four Democratic-Republican candidates ran against each other. Andrew Jackson won the popular vote and ninety-nine electoral votes. However, the lack of an electoral majority threw the election to the House of Representatives, which ended up giving the victory to John Quincy Adams.

New York Senator Martin van Buren began working on a party, the Democratic Party, which backed Jackson in 1828 who defeated Adams. Andrew Jackson is the first Democrat president of the USA.[50] Jackson was our first President from west of the Appalachian Mountains. A hero of the War of 1812, Battle of New Orleans, Jackson was responsible for the Trail of Tears and supported slavery. The Trail of Tears is the common name given to forced relocation of the Native tribes of the southeast to west of the Mississippi River. Several positive aspects of Jacksonian ideals were that he was a Unionist and he campaigned for and succeeded in giving the vote to all white men. As a Unionist, Jackson would have given up on slavery rather than break up the Union. If Andrew Jackson were alive in 1860, he likely would have been an influence against succession. By giving the vote to all white men, the possibility of abolishing slavery was greatly increased. As mentioned previously, each state began developing a legal system while the nation was at war with Great Britain. As such the vote was predominantly granted to white, male property owners who were 21 years or older, as was British custom.

MEXICAN AMERICAN WAR

The tenuous balancing act continued, and westward expansion continued with more territories organized in the lands of the Louisiana Purchase. America's third Democrat President, James K Polk was elected in 1844. Polk believed the USA had a "Manifest Destiny" to span from coast to coast. Polk had proposed that the US:

1. Annex Texas as a slave state.
2. Occupy Oregon, which was then part of Canada.
3. Pursue what is now the American southwest, part of then Mexico.

Mexican cavalry attacked the disputed territory of Texas, and the Mexican American War was on. The US eventually prevailed, and the war ended with the Treaty of

Guadalupe Hidalgo on February 2, 1848. The terms of this treaty included:

1. The Mexican American border was established as the Rio Grande River.
2. Mexico recognizing the annexation of Texas by the US
3. Mexico sells the balance of lands north of the Rio Grande for $15 million.

The Mexican American War was over but the battle over slavery continued. Northern abolitionists attacked the war as an attempt by slave owners to strengthen the power of slave proponents.[51] The abolitionist House, which considered the war a land grab, wanted to outlaw slavery in the new territory. The Senate blocked these efforts with the Wilmot Proviso.[52, 53]

All or a majority of the following seven states were eventually carved from the territory relinquished in the Treaty of Guadalupe Hidalgo:

1. Arizona
2. California
3. Colorado
4. Nevada
5. New Mexico
6. Texas (recognized in treaty)
7. Utah

That certainly would have upset the balance of power.

DRED SCOTT V. SANFORD

In April 1846, Dred and Harriet filed separate lawsuits for freedom in the St. Louis Circuit Court based on two Missouri statutes. The first statute allowed any person of any color to sue for wrongful enslavement. The second stated that any person taken to a free territory automatically became free and could not be re-enslaved upon returning to a slave state.

Dred and Harriet Scott were illiterate. They needed both logistical and financial support to plead their case. They received that support from their church, abolitionists and one unlikely source, the Blow family who had once owned them.

Dred and Harriet Scott had lived in Illinois and the Wisconsin Territory where slavery was illegal by the Northwest Ordinances. They hoped they had a persuasive case for freedom. They went to trial on June 30, 1847, unfortunately, the court ruled against them on a technicality and the judge granted a retrial.

After numerous legal actions in state and federal courts the case came before the US Supreme Court. On March 6, 1857, in the infamous Dred Scott decision, Dred Scott lost his fight for freedom again. Roger Taney, the Chief Justice of the Supreme Court of the United States wrote the majority decision. In his decision Taney asserted that, all people of African descent, free or enslaved, were not United States citizens and therefore had no right to sue in federal court. He also wrote that the Fifth Amendment protected slave owner rights because enslaved people were their legal property. Taney also asserted that the prohibitions against slavery in the Northwest Ordinance and Missouri Compromise were unconstitutional.[54]

Roger Taney was nominated as Chief Justice by President Andrew Jackson. He served as Chief justice from March 28, 1836, to October 12, 1864. As a stroke of irony, Taney swore in "The Great Emancipator" Abraham Lincoln as our first Republican and 16th President of the USA.[55]

THE COMPROMISE OF 1850

"Pharaoh's Country was cursed with plagues, and his hosts were drowned in the Red Sea for striving to retain a captive people who had already served them four hundred years. May like disasters never befall us!" Abraham Lincoln, July 6th, 1852[56]

Another attempt at avoiding national discord over slavery was the Compromise of 1850. Senator Clay of Kentucky again attempted to compromise in 1850. This bill was championed by Senator Daniel Webster of Massachusetts though he did not support expansion of slavery into the newly acquired territories. As a result, he disappointed his abolitionist supporters. This was an effort to avoid the inevitable, a civil war.

Aging and in ill health, as Clay began to fail, the cause was taken up by Illinois Senator, Democrat Steven Douglas a proponent of states' rights over slavery.

MAIN POINTS OF THE COMPROMISE OF 1850

The Compromise of 1850 was made up of five separate bills that made the following main points:

1. Slavery was permitted in Washington, DC, but outlawed the slave trade.
2. California was added to the Union as a "free state."
3. Utah and New Mexico were established as territories that could decide via popular sovereignty if they would permit slavery.
4. New boundaries were defined for the state of Texas following the Mexican American War, removing its claims to parts of New Mexico but awarding the state $10 million in compensation
5. The Fugitive Slave Act of 1850 required citizens to assist in apprehending runaway slaves and denied enslaved people a right to trial by jury.

The Fugitive Slave Act of 1850 required all citizens to assist in the capture of runaways and denied enslaved people the right to a jury trial. It also established federal commissioners to control individual cases. These federal commissioners were paid more for returning a suspected slave than for freeing them. The law obviously was biased in favor of Southern slave holders.

The resultant outrage only increased traffic along the Underground Railroad during the 1850s. Northern states avoided enforcing the law and by 1860 only about 330 run-aways were successfully returned.[57]

It was clear the southern slave interests were not going to accept a true compromise.

KANSAS NEBRASKA ACT OF 1854

"Whereas, Slavery, throughout its entire existence in the United States is none other than a most barbarous, unprovoked, and unjustifiable War of one portion of its citizens upon another portion; the only conditions of which are perpetual imprisonment, and hopeless servitude or absolute extermination; in utter disregard and violation of those eternal and self-evident truths set forth in our Declaration of Independence." John Brown[58]

In January 1854, Senator Stephen Douglas of Illinois introduced a bill that divided the land immediately west of Missouri into two territories, Kansas and Nebraska. This bill would overturn the hard-won anti-slavery provisions of the Missouri Compromise of 1820. Under the terms of the Missouri Compromise of 1820, slavery would have been outlawed in both territories since they were both north of the 36°30' N dividing line between "slave" and "free" states. Douglass argued in favor of popular sovereignty, or the idea that the settlers of the new territories should decide if slavery would be legal there.

After months of debate, the Kansas-Nebraska Act passed on May 30, 1854. This resulted in pro-slavery and anti-slavery settlers rushing to Kansas. Both sides hoping to win the first election held. Many skirmishes between abolitionist and pro-slavery settlers resulted in the term "Bleeding Kansas". John Brown's legend as a militant abolitionist was just beginning. John Brown's efforts in Kansas continued for several years. During this time, several sons were captured by pro-slavery forces and one son killed. Brown continued to advocate for the movement, traveling around the country to raise money and weapons for the cause. In 1859 Kansas voted to be a free state.[59] The act aggravated the split between North and South on the issue of slavery until reconciliation seemed virtually impossible.[60]

FOUNDING OF THE REPUBLICAN PARTY

The Republican party was founded in "The Little White School House" in Ripon Wisconsin on March 20, 1854, from the abolitionist remnants of the Whig party and Free-Soil Democrats. This action resulted in a realignment of the major political parties on the issue of slavery. The anti-slavery, pro individual freedom forces consolidated in the Republican party. Likewise, the pro-slavery, "we can control other people's lives" forces consolidated in the Democrat party. In both parties there was a spectrum of thought from the extremes of position.[61, 62]

UNCLE TOM'S CABIN INCITES ABOLITIONIST SENTIMENTS

The original title was *Uncle Tom's Cabin or Life Among the Lowly*. The popularity of Uncle Tom's Cabin along with the Fugitive Slave Laws fueled a rise of abolitionist sentiments in the north. To many in today's America the term Uncle Tom is used as a pejorative. A term to indicate someone is subservient and will not stand up for themselves. In fact, Uncle Tom was the hero of the story.

When Harriet Beecher Stowe wrote Uncle Tom's Cabin, she intended to present the cruelties of slavery many northern whites did not fully appreciate. Stowe also included a message that slavery could be overcome by Christian love. Uncle Tom's Cabin was first published in an abolitionist periodical, The National Review. This release occurred as a 40-week serial beginning June 5, 1851, with the last episode released April 1, 1852. Uncle Tom's Cabin was also published in book form with the first release March 20, 1852. Subsequent printings were made until the late 1800's. The book ultimately had impact around the world.

Harriet Beecher Stowe attempted to portray the injustice and brutality of slavery. The story portrays the relationships within the slave population and between slaves and their masters. Uncle Tom, the main character, is portrayed as a noble, Christian slave. In each situation Tom is the self-sacrificing servant helping others. Unfortunately, due to financial situations Tom is sold to pay off debts. His final master is the cruel Simon Legree who intends to demoralize Tom and break him of his

Christian faith. As the story draws to a close two young slave girls plan an escape. They realize they likely could not outrun the slave trackers and dogs. The girls devise a plan to hide in a crate in the attic of the big house. They would wait in the crate until the ruckus quiets down then sneak away in the night. Tom is aware of their plan and Simon Legree decides since he is a respected slave, the girls must have confided their plans with him. Legree had his overseer, an African named Sambo, whip Tom until he died. In the end Tom was interpreted by the northern public as a Christ-like image of the suffering servant.

It has been reported that when Harriet Beecher Stowe visited President Lincoln he stated, "So, this is the little lady who started this great war."[63]

It was reported that Queen Victoria wept when she read Uncle Tom's Cabin. Both northern and southern Democrats expressed violent responses including mob violence, burning mailbags of abolitionist literature, and passage of a "gag rule" banning anti-slavery petitions in the US House of Representatives.[64, 65, 66]

For many extremist Republicans, the Civil War was of a holy war. Armed with the Christ-like image of Uncle Tom as the suffering servant, early in the war Union troops went to battle singing an improvised tune honoring the abolitionist hero John Brown.

John Brown's body lies a-mouldering in the grave
John Brown's body lies a-mouldering in the grave
John Brown's body lies a-mouldering in the grave

His soul's marching on
Glory, hallelujah, Glory, hallelujah, Glory, hallelujah

HIS SOUL IS MARCHING ON

Abolitionist, Julia Ward Howe first heard this song during a public review of the troops outside Washington, DC. The Reverend James Freeman Clarke accompanied Howe at the review and suggested that she write new words for the men's fight song. After a sound night's sleep at the Willard Hotel Howe awoke and began to write the verses to the "Battle Hymn of the Republic."[67]

Mine eyes have seen the glory of the coming of the Lord;
He is trampling out the vintage where the grapes of
wrath are stored;
He hath loosed the fateful lightning of His terrible
swift sword:
His truth is marching on.
(Chorus)
Glory, glory, hallelujah!
Glory, glory, hallelujah!
Glory, glory, hallelujah!
His truth is marching on. (first verse)[68]

CHAPTER 3

THE CIVIL WAR AND RECONSTRUCTION

The previous chapter portrays the struggle legislatively and sometimes violently, over the issue of slavery in the early years of the USA. Many founding fathers believed the slavery issue would ultimately lead to civil war. It is not my intent to include extensive details of civil war battle history but to include some details I had not learned previously.

Abe Lincoln our first Republican President was elected with 39.8 percent of the popular vote but 59.4 percent of the electoral vote. In 1860 the Democrat Party was split on whether to secede. Steven Douglass, the Northern Democrat, was the pro-slavery candidate but did not support certain expansion to new territories. John Breckenridge, the Southern Democrat, was pro-slavery and wanted slavery to expand to new territories. Combined, Steven Douglass and John Breckenridge received 47.6 percent of the popular vote but only 27.7 percent of the electoral vote. A fourth party the Constitutional Union party selected John Bell who received 12.6 percent of the popular vote and 12.8 percent of the electoral vote. Abraham

Lincoln was not on the ballet in any southern state.[1,2] Was that because it was not safe to register in those states? I could only speculate.

By the time of Lincoln's Inauguration on March 4, 1861, seven southern states had seceded. Abraham Lincoln was a Unionist and wanted to preserve the Union. He closed his first inaugural address with the following plea:

> "I am loath to close. We are not enemies, but friends. We must not be enemies. Though passion may have strained it must not break our bonds of affection. The mystic chords of memory, stretching from every battlefield and patriot grave to every living heart and hearthstone all over this broad land, will yet swell the chorus of the Union, when again touched, as surely they will be, by the better angels of our nature."[3]

Unfortunately, the South attacked Fort Sumter on April 12th, 1861, and our nation began its bloodiest war.

What contribution did native Americans have during the Civil War? Members of the "Five Civilized Tribes" fought on both sides of the American Civil War, Union and Confederate divisions within the tribes were deep during the war. The tribes were considered separate nations by treaty and as such, the Emancipation Proclamation or agreements between the North and South did not apply. However, post war treaties eliminated slavery within the tribal nations.[4]

IT DIDN'T END AT APPOMATTOX

My history class taught that General Robert E Lee surrendered to General Ulysses S Grant at Appomattox Courthouse and the Union captured Richmond ending the war. However, Jefferson Davis' government officials had fled Richmond and were on the run for nearly a month after Lee's surrender. The South still had standing armies that had not yet surrendered. Jefferson Davis called for the South to fight on applying guerrilla tactics. Fortunately, Davis was captured on May 9th,1865.[5] The last confederate general to surrender was Cherokee Chief Stand Watie on June 23rd, 1865.[6] The final Confederate surrender of the war did not occur until November 6, 1865, when Captain James Waddell's ship CSS *Shenandoah* reached Liverpool England and was surrendered to British authorities. The *Shenandoah* had sunk several Union ships after the hostilities had been concluded and the Confederate government dissolved. Captain Waddell surrendered the *Shenandoah* to the British to avoid being hung as a pirate in the USA. Also, the ship had originated as an English commercial vessel.[7, 8] Teddy Roosevelt's, uncle, Irvine Bulloch, was the sailing master for this voyage.[9] Three decades later Teddy would become the 26th US President. As we will see TR made strides in helping "black improvement."

RECONSTRUCTION

The period between the end of the Civil War and the election of 1876 is known as the Reconstruction Era. During this period, the KKK and other white supremacist groups formed throughout the south. These groups arose to resist Republican efforts to ensure civil rights, provide for education and economic opportunities for the freed slaves, and suffrage for black men.[10] As a result, the Union and General Grant were forced to maintain federal troops in the South as an occupying force to maintain order. This occupation was not well received by the southern Democrats who ten to fifteen years earlier had rebelled against the Union to maintain slavery. To reestablish good standing in the Union, southern states had to pledge acceptance and support of the new laws and constitutional amendments written to protect the formerly enslaved people.

By the time, the 1876 election arrived the North was growing tired of having to maintain a permanent occupying force in the South. During the election of 1876, Democrats in three southern states, South Carolina, Florida, and Louisiana, attempted to establish their own parallel state government with armed rifle companies formed to take over the state government from the Republican state government backed by the federal government.[11] Had the South truly accepted the dissolution of the Confederacy? As a result, two slates of presidential electors were sent to Washington, DC, from each of these three states. One sent by the legitimate, supported Republican government and one from the renegade Democrat government. Wanting to maintain a sense of neutrality, President Grant did not send federal troops to defend the legitimate governments. President Grant, to a great extent, did not get involved in efforts of Congress to unravel this mess and determine the next president in time for a March 4th inauguration.

The candidates in this election were Republican Rutherford B. Hayes from Ohio and Democrat Samuel J Tilden of New York. If the Republican slate of electors for the three states in dispute are used Rutherford B Hayes is president. Likewise, if the Democrat slate of electors is used Samuel J Tilden is president. The final agreement was Hayes would be president and the Union would withdraw Federal troops from the South.[12] The South promised to respect the rights of recently freed slaves, which did not happen. As Woodrow Wilson put it, "the mischief of reconstruction" ended hence Jim Crow began or continued. Woodrow Wilson was elected in 1912 as our first Progressive Democrat President and was an apologist for the institution of slavery. Wilson described slavery as a "benevolent state" for Negroes, whose white masters looked after their "comfort and welfare," and "meted out justice fairly." [13] This should not be surprising after you realize Woodrow Wilson is the only US president to have been a citizen of the Confederacy. The policies he invoked displayed his beliefs as will be discussed shortly.

From its founding this nation was divided on the issue of slavery. The history during the early years of expansion showed a constant effort to maintain balance. The pro-slavery forces defended their institution; the pro-freedom forces resisted slavery and there were many violent clashes between both sides.

Thomas Sowell has made the following observations.

> "If slavery is not morally wrong it is hard to imagine what else could possibly be wrong" yet when Lincoln expressed this view which was gaining currency in his time it was a belief less than a century old in the west and still virtually non-existent outside the West. In ancient times Aristotle had attempted to justify slavery. But many other Western and non-western philosophers alike took it so much for granted that they felt no need to explain or justify it at all...
>
> Only in the American South did a large apologetic literature develop seeking to justify slavery because only there was slavery under such large scale and sustained attacks on moral grounds as to require a response.
>
> While slavery was referred to in antebellum America as a peculiar institution, in an international perspective and in the "Long View of History" it was not this institution that was peculiar but the principles of American Freedom with which slavery was in such obvious and irreconcilable conflict.[14, 15]

The institution of slavery exists because of human greed, arrogance, selfishness, and sin. In the United States people spent a lot of time justifying why they enslaved others. These efforts were made to convince others they were justified in this injustice. It may well be a salve for a guilty conscience. Whatever the reason, the result was demeaning to those enslaved. They were denied their dignity. In the United States this took the form of assigning the enslaved to some contrived lower form of being. I've heard this referred to as the "othering" of an individual. Slavery is a power struggle; one group of people taking advantage of others. Bogus science has been used to denigrate diverse groups as well, not just blacks. We'll have more on this in the next chapter. As years passed, some in the south and elsewhere began to think the war did not end in 1865, but rather the war came to an end with the end of Reconstruction.

CHAPTER 4
SYSTEMIC RACISM

One narrative I had heard to justify slavery was that the Africans were simple childlike creatures unable to direct their own lives. This argument included the proviso that if they resisted their enslavement, they were mentally unstable. On the face of it, this argument is illogical and easily refuted. The "science" had to be refined.

HARVARD AND SCIENTIFIC RACISM

In 1846, the renowned Swiss naturalist, Louis Agasi, gave a speech before 5000 people in Boston. This his first American lecture was titled "The Plan of Creation in the Animal Kingdom". When Agasi arrived in America he believed in the theory that all humans descended from a single creation derived from the biblical creation story. After he met Dr. Samuel Morton of Philadelphia, one of America's most distinguished scientists, he began to rethink his position and accept the theories of Dr. Morton. Agasi accepted a professorship at Harvard and head of the Lawrence Scientific School.[1]

CHAPTER 4: SYSTEMIC RACISM

UNIVERSITY OF PENNSYLVANIA AND SCIENTIFIC RACISM

Dr. Morton, a Philadelphia physician, had the world's largest collection of human skulls which he used to investigate the innate differences among humans by looking at skull size and volume. While a professor at Penn Medical College Morton published "Crania Americana" in 1839. In this work Morton described the "Ethiopian Race" as:

"Characterized by a black complexion...the negro is joyous, flexible and indolent: while the many nations which compose this race present a singular diversity of intellectual character of which the far extreme is the lowest grade of humanity."[2]

Morton believed he could scientifically document the superiority of certain races by taking these skull measurements. Morton was not alone in this study, many scientists in North America and Europe were following the same thinking. He was using science to document his own philosophical and political biases. Southern plantation owners love this idea as science was supporting their position. A majority of early Penn Medical School graduates were from Southern slave holding states; those would be folks who had the finances and spare time.[3, 4, 5]

I thought this concept seemed strange when I first heard of the technique. The research I previously heard of occurred nearly one hundred years later. During the 1930's Nazi scientists were scouring the planet for the origins of the Aryan race using similar methods. In both instances scientists were corrupting the scientific method to support flawed pre-conceptions. It is also significant that the scientists promoting this concept rejected the creation worldview of the Judeo-Christian and Islamic traditions.

FROM ACROSS THE POND

Darwin published his "On the Origin of Species by Means of Natural Selection, or the Preservation of Favoured Races in the Struggle for Life" (the complete original title) in 1859.[6] Darwin's cousin Francis Galton followed with the promotion of eugenics.

Francis Galton made contributions in many fields of knowledge; however, eugenics was his primary interest. Galton devoted the latter part of his life to promoting the idea that the physical and mental makeup of the human species could be improved by selective breeding and parenthood. Galton quickly recognized the implications of the theory of evolution for humankind. He believed it invalidated much of contemporary theology. For Galton evolution also opened possibilities for planned improvement of the human species.

Galton coined the word *eugenics* to denote scientific endeavors to increase the proportion of persons with better than average genetic endowment through selective mating of marriage partners. Galton published "Hereditary Genius" (1869). He used the word genius to denote "an ability that was exceptionally high and at the same time inborn." He argued that mental and physical characteristics are equally inherited, a concept that was controversial at the time.[7]

It was reported that after reading his book Darwin wrote his cousin saying, "You have made a convert of an opponent in one sense for I have always maintained that, excepting fools, men did not differ much in intellect, only in zeal and hard work." Galton was not mentioned in his book "Origin of Species" in 1859. Darwin however drew on Galton's thoughts quoting him several times in Darwin's "Descent of Man" (1871).

Galton's belief that mental as well as physical traits are inherited shaped his religious beliefs.[8] "We cannot doubt the existence of a great power ready to hand and capable of being directed with vast benefit as soon as we have learned to understand and apply it."[9]

Galton's ideals were embraced by the elites of American society and higher education. Eugenics were the foundational science for the American Birth Control League and as a justification for forced sterilizations.[10] Many of the concepts of American eugenicists were embraced by Nazi scientists.

RECONSTRUCTION—JIM CROW

During reconstruction the freed slaves made tremendous progress. Many started businesses, historically black colleges were founded, primary schools were established for education of the freed slaves, and many were elected to political offices both locally and in Washington, DC. Reconstruction ended with the presidential election of 1876. Union troops had remained in the South to maintain order and ensure the civil rights of the freed slaves. This had been a very contested election with Rutherford B. Hayes the would-be the President and Union troops to be withdrawn from the South. There was also the promise that the South would respect the civil rights of the freed slaves.

Instead, what happened were Jim Crow laws, black codes, pole taxes, voter suppression and violence against the black population. Despite southern resistance much progress was made. Many historically black colleges and universities were established. The black community developed a thriving parallel economy. Black people attained lower level and supervisory positions in the federal government.

TEDDY ROOSEVELT -BULLY

The McKinley/Roosevelt ticket won the election of 1900 by a landslide. Teddy Roosevelt was concerned his political career would be derailed as VP, but on September 6, 1901, an assassin shot President McKinley at the Pan-American Exposition in Buffalo NY. At 2:15 a.m. on September 14, 1901, President McKinley succumbed to his injuries. Roosevelt, who had been in transit, arrived to learn of McKinley's death. A US district judge administered the oath of office at 3:00 p.m. at the Ansley Wilcox House.

At the age of forty-two, Teddy Roosevelt (TR) was the youngest to serve as president. As a Progressive Republican, TR began implementing his "Square Deal" making the government work for the common man as well as the elites. Roosevelt's efforts included breaking up bad trusts, regulation of pure food and drugs, as well as rail-roads. Roosevelt worked to preserve the nation's resources, founded national parks, forests, and monuments. He was also interested in projecting American strength and influence around the world and constructed the Panama Canal.

The Roosevelt family was part of Ward McCallister's the "Four Hundred" best families of New York City high society. Roosevelt embraced a strenuous lifestyle as a rancher in North Dakota. Roosevelt gained national fame as war hero leading his Rough Riders in the Spanish-American War. Roosevelt's father had instilled in him a sense of duty to serve his fellow man. Despite being a scion of the "Four Hundred," TR was a decent man who believed in equality.

Some years before, TR had befriended Booker T. Washington, former slave and founder of the Tuskegee Institute and national leader in African American circles. They had been consulting about how to improve the position of the African American community. Washington had been researching and recommending African American candidates for government posts as part of TR's best man for the job policy.[11]

On October 16, 1901, the new president invited his friend Booker T. to meet, talk politics and have dinner at 7:30 p.m.

This was not uncharacteristic for TR as he had invited African Americans to dinner during his brief stint as New York Governor. Dinner included the entire Roosevelt family and an additional guest. After an evening of fine dining and productive political discussions Booker T. said good night.[12]

The next day the White House release a statement titled: "Booker T. Washington of Tuskegee, Alabama, dined with the President last evening." Soon the telegraphs began clicking, spreading the news across the country. Shortly afterward, criticism came from all over the South. TR had committed a great affront to their southern sensibilities. The South condemned Roosevelt as a traitor to the believers in white superiority.[13]

TR was an educated man of his times, a Harvard graduate and a member of the elite of society with an active inquisitive mind. Thomas G. Dyer wrote of TR: "The force of race in history occupied a singularly important place in Roosevelt's broad intellectual outlook."[14]

Additionally, Roosevelt believed fundamentally that the greatness of America was the result of rule by racially superior white men of European descent. Remember, TR's mother was a southern woman with the southern "sensibilities" of the day. I suspect she had great influence on these racial ideas. However, TR was also familiar with the science of Charles Darwin and Jean-Baptiste Lamarck.

According to Michael Patrick Cullinane, "Roosevelt believed that individuals could learn positive traits within their lifetime and assumed racial mobility was within human control."[15]

Biographer Edmund Morris claimed Roosevelt *"admired individual achievement above all things."*[16]

Booker T. Washington's achievements would have been greatly admired by TR. It's said that after the meeting with Booker T., TR wrote: "The only wise and honorable and Christian thing to do is to treat each black man and each white man strictly on his merits as a man, giving him no more and no less than he shows himself worthy to have."[17]

Forty-four years after TR's death Dr. Martin Luther King Jr. stated, "I have a dream that my four little children will one day live in a nation where they will not be judged by the color of their skin but by the content of their character."[18]

WOODROW WILSON AND JIM CROW PROGRESSIVISM

After serving as Teddy Roosevelt's vice president, William Howard Taft was elected president in 1908 as a Republican. Taft governed in a far more conservative manner than Roosevelt cared for. Roosevelt then founded an opposition Republican Party called Bull Moose. Woodrow Wilson was the Progressive nominee of the Democrat Party. The result was a race between the three major candidates. The Republicans vote split between Taft and Roosevelt. The incumbent, Taft received 23.2 percent of the popular vote and 1.5 percent of the electoral vote. TR received 27.4 percent of the popular vote and 16.6 percent of the electoral vote. Woodrow Wilson won the election with about 42 percent of the popular vote and 81.9 percent of the electoral vote.[19]

During the campaign Wilson had courted prominent members of the black community indicating that he would support their cause.[20] However, after the election Woodrow Wilson resegregated many government departments including the Treasury, the Post Office, the Bureau of Engraving and Printing, the Navy, the Interior, the Marine Hospital, the War Department and the Government Printing Office. The Postal Service was the largest department with offices across the country and many blacks were fired or demoted.[21] Wilson's action reversed hard fought economic progress by African Americans from Reconstruction through William Howard Taft. It's my belief that the historical lexicon should include the term Jim Crow Progressivism.

Woodrow Wilson viewed the first movie shown in the White House. The movie, *The Birth of a Nation*, was based on the stage play titled, *The Clansman* written by Thomas Dixon.[22, 23] Wilson endorsed the film saying, "It is like writing history with lightning, and my only regret is that it is all so terribly true."[24]

Wilson and Dixon met at Johns Hopkins University where they were studying history.[25] Wilson received his doctorate in history from Johns Hopkins. *Birth of a Nation*, a silent movie, portrayed black men as animalistic rapists and the Ku Klux Klan as the defenders of white womanhood.

Until recently I thought silent movies were always

accompanied by piano music until I learned there was an orchestral score written. The composer, Joseph Carl Breil, included snare drums, bugles, along with a full orchestra for an extremely dramatic effect.[26, 27] I'm sure there was a piano score for small theaters. However, in a large city with a symphony orchestra, a great, possibly emotionally charged spectacle would be created; remember the cinema was new tech and impressive. This was also Woodrow Wilson's history coming to life.

Another early innovation of the early 1900s is the theatrical organ. Theater organs came into prominence during the era of silent films. Theatrical organs avoided the expense of a complete orchestra. One musician could simulate the effect of an orchestra. In additional to the ranks of an organ, theatrical organs included percussion, wind instruments, xylophones, wood harps, chimes, sleigh bells, chrysoglotts, and glockenspiels.[28, 29] I was fortunate to have enjoyed a concert on a theater organ; it was spectacular. Check these out.[30, 31, 32]

Race relations during the Wilson administration declined significantly. Historians have written about many clashes which were referred to as race riots. I think the more appropriate term would be massacre. The summer of 1919 saw incidents across the country.[33] Other incidents include Tulsa Black Wall Street in 1921,[34] and the massacre in Rosewood, Florida[35] in 1923.

When I first heard of Woodrow Wilson's racial history (around 2005) and the movie *Birth of a Nation*, I was dumbfounded that we had not been taught anything of that history in the 1960s. During that time, we had a neighbor who had participated in local civil rights protests in the 1960s. As a black man some 20 years older than myself, I was sure he would have known about Wilson. When I asked, he also was surprised, and said that he would speak with somebody he knew. When I enquired a short while later, my neighbor said his contact confirmed that Woodrow Wilson was not a friend of the black community. Earlier I mentioned my thoughts on who was writing the history at the time. I believe the history being taught was a neo-Confederate "Lost Cause" movement. However, by the time I was in public school in the 1960s, there was no mention of Woodrow Wilson's wrong doings. If you control the writing of history, you can present the story in whatever manner you choose.

Woodrow Wilson's treasury secretary and eventual son-in-law, William Gibbs McAdoo, ran for President in 1924. McAdoo received support from temperance supporters and the KKK. During the 1924 Democratic convention in New York McAdoo's forces railed against the anti-Klan forces supporting the New York Reformer, Al Smith. The two side had fist fights at the convention. After 103 votes Smith's side lost by one vote. Neither side had achieved the required two-thirds vote required. Being hopelessly deadlocked the two sides settled on a conservative attorney for JP Morgan, John W. David. Neither faction got their way. With the economy booming David was crushed by Calvin Coolidge in the election. I was surprised that the KKK of the Jim Crow Progressive Era often served as enforcers of prohibition with concern for the "morals" of society among other progressive causes.[36, 37]

By 1925 the public became disenchanted with stories of corruption, immorality, and violence of a group that championed American womanhood, Christianity, and prohibition. The public began to reject the KKK and soon Klan membership declined from nearly 4 million in 1925 to less than 200,000 by 1928.[38]

The Progressive Era ran from roughly 1880s to the early 1920s. During my 1960s history classes we had been told the public tired of Progressive Policies. The curriculum did not include the corrupt, violent aspect of Klan history in the early 1900s. We had only news of the 1960s Klan to reflect on.

I wonder how much of the population was influenced by the pseudo-science of eugenics. I am confident it was popular with the ruling class who was planning the development of the nation. Woodrow Wilson and the "experts" he brought into government were fundamentalist in their application of eugenics; science that justified the southern social structure they wished to preserve, and in the parlance of today they found confirmation bias in Eugenics.

FROM THE HARVARD REVIEW

The scientific method developed in Europe as an outgrowth of western civilization. Most of the early scientists such as Sir Isaac Newton believed they were working to discover the secrets of God's creation. By the late 1800s the progressive elites of American society wanted to show they had created a nation to be reckoned with, a nation as great as any in Europe. As such they were enamored with this science that identified them as being of "superior stock," white, northern European protestants.

By 1900, the educated elites of American society widely accepted the concept of eugenics, regardless of political affiliation. As mentioned previously Francis Galton's eugenics was a branch from his cousin, Charles Darwin's "Theory of Evolution." As such it is fair to assume many who rejected evolution rejected eugenics as well.

Former Harvard president Charles William Eliot addressed the Harvard Club of San Francisco in August of 1912. His topic was a subject close to his heart—racial purity. Eliot declared America was being threatened by immigration of a mixture of racial groups which he thought could bring about a grave danger. Eliot told his San Francisco audience, "Each nation should keep its stock pure," and "There should be no blending of races."[39]

Eliot's concern for race mixing included Catholics marrying white Anglo-Saxon Protestants, Jews marrying Gentiles, and non-whites marrying whites, all of which violated the central tenet of eugenics. The eugenics movement in Europe and the United States, insisted that human progress depended on promoting reproduction by the best people in the best combinations, and preventing the unworthy from having children.[40]

Another major eugenic cause which Eliot promoted was forced sterilization of people declared to be "feebleminded," physically disabled, "criminalistic," or otherwise flawed. This included the gay community as homosexuality was considered a mental illness. Indiana had enacted the nation's first eugenic sterilization law in 1907. In 1911 Eliot wrote a paper on "The Suppression of Moral Defectives," and praised Indiana's law as it "blazed the trail which all free states must follow, if they would protect themselves from moral degeneracy." This legislation was passed by a Republican legislature and signed into law by a Republican Governor, Frank Hanley.[41] Also, in 1907 Woodrow Wilson campaigned in Indiana for compulsory sterilization of criminals and the mentally retarded.[42, 43]

This former Harvard president and professor enthusiastically joined a campaign to build a global eugenics movement. Eliot served as vice president of the First International Eugenics Congress, held in London in 1912. During this conference papers were presented on "racial suicide" among Northern Europeans and related topics. In 1914, Eliot helped organize the First National Conference on Race Betterment in Battle Creek, Michigan.[44]

Eugenics was well-established with in the intellectual mainstream at the university. Harvard administrators, faculty members, and alumni were at the forefront of American eugenics. Harvard influence was felt in founding eugenics organizations, writing academic and popular eugenics articles. After all they have always been at the tip of the spear of American science. As a leading institution in the Progressive movement where educated elites were trained to plan society, they also lobbied government to enact eugenics laws.[45]

The eugenics movement included some of New England's oldest families dating back to before the American Revolution. Oliver Wendell Holmes Sr. embraced eugenics and was dean of Harvard Medical School, an acclaimed writer, and father of the future Supreme Court Justice Holmes, whose ancestors had been attending Harvard since John Oliver entered in 1680. Holmes had been writing about human breeding before Galton. Holmes coined the phrase "Boston Brahmin" in an 1861 book in which he described his social class as "a physical and mental elite, identifiable by its noble "physiognomy" and "aptitude for learning,"[46] which he insisted were "congenital and hereditary."

Some other enthusiastic academic institutions mentioned in the Harvard Magazine article referenced are Stanford's first president, David Starr Jordan, Yale's economist, Irving Fisher, The University of Virginia professor Robert Bennett Bean.[47] But how about other Ivy League institutions? As previously discussed, historians of this period such as William Archibald Dunning at Columbia University, and Woodrow Wilson, Princeton professor, university president, New Jersey governor and President of the United States, told a neo-Confederate history of the "Lost Cause" which fits supports the same philosophy.[48]

In the end the Harvard Magazine article states that, "It is understandable that the University (Harvard) is not eager to recall its part in that tragically misguided intellectual movement—but it is a chapter too important to be forgotten."[49]

I would take issue that the "promotion of eugenics" was not forgotten but rather was deliberately hidden for decades if not generations. I take this article as more of a clandestine confession. It must have been deliberately hidden since this Ivy League science was the groundwork for their eugenics successors in Germany–the Nazis.

Not discussed in the Harvard Magazine article is the fact that the policies implemented were part of the early Progressives public health policy; a totalitarian health system intended to improve the nations "human stock" by eliminating those they considered defective mentally, morally, or racially.

Another topic not discussed in the Harvard Review Article is the "One Drop Rule" which was codified into state laws in the early 1900s. The "One Drop Rule" asserted that a person was black if they had any African ancestry. The main purpose of the "One Drop Rule" was to prevent inter-racial marriage or misogyny. Prior to the advent of eugenics, a person's blackness was defined by a fraction of black ancestry. For example, an octaroon was one-eighth black having one great grandparent; a quadroon was one-fourth black having one grandparent. Likewise, a quintaroon was one-sixteenth black having one great-great grandparent. A mulatto was a person with one black parent. The laws varied from state to state.[50]

As George D Tillman of South Carolina stated in 1895:

"It is a scientific fact that there is not one full-blooded Caucasian on the floor of this convention. Every member has in him a certain mixture of . . . colored blood. . . It would be a cruel injustice and the source of endless litigation, of scandal, horror, feud, and bloodshed to undertake to annul or forbid marriage for a remote, perhaps obsolete trace of Negro blood. The doors would be open to scandal, malice, and greed."[51]

As eugenics was promoted in American universities, state laws became even more extreme. Tennessee was the first state to codify the "One Drop Rule" in 1910 but others followed.

State	Year
Texas	1911
Arkansas	1911
Mississippi	1917
North Carolina	1923
Alabama	1927
Georgia	1927
Oklahoma	1933

Other states tightened the blood fraction statutes to one-sixteenth or one thirty-second, basically a one drop rule.[52] I don't know of records that tie the students of Dr. Morton in Philadelphia to Jim Crow Progressivism, however, it seems reasonable to think they are connected, like father like son, like grandson. Could it be the Jim Crow Progressive movement has roots in southern plantation culture?

Eugenics is an example of what Richard Feynman called Cargo Cult Science in 1972. Feynman pointed out:

"There are areas of study referred to as science that never yield a result, in effect they are a pseudoscience."

"There are big schools of reading methods and mathematics methods, and so forth, but if you notice, you'll see the reading scores keep going down—or hardly going up—in spite of the fact that we continually use these same people to improve the methods"

"Another example is how to treat criminals. We obviously have made no progress—lots of theory, but no progress—in decreasing the amount of crime by the method that we use to handle criminals."

"Yet these things are said to be scientific. We study them. And I think ordinary people with commonsense ideas are intimidated by this pseudoscience. A teacher who has some good idea of how to teach her children to read is forced by the school system to do it some other way—or is even fooled by the school system into thinking that her method is not necessarily a good one. Or a parent of bad boys, after disciplining them in one way or another, feels guilty for the rest of her life because she didn't do 'the right thing,' according to the experts."[53]

In the case of eugenics, it is a theory that confirms pre-conceived notions of its proponents. When presenting an idea for scrutiny all possibilities for or against should be presented. This allows the reviewers a chance to test all hypothesis.[54]

During high school history class in the 1960s we were not told of any contributions of black Americans to the progress of the nation. I believe it was during this period that the Jim Crow Progressive Era contributions of black Americans to the building of this nation were erased from history curricula. A brief list includes:

1. Crispus Attucks, a black man was the first American casualty of the Revolutionary War and an early member of the anti-slavery movement[55]
2. Black Soldiers comprised as much as 10 percent of George Washington's Continental Army[56]
3. Inventions by black Americans which include:[57]
   a. Folding Cabinet Bed
   b. Potato Chips
   c. Multiplex Telegraph
   d. Shoe Lasting Machine
   e. Automatic Oil Cup
   f. Carbon-filament Light Bulb
   g. Walker Hair Care System
   h. Blood Bank
   i. Protective Mailbox
   j. Gas Mask
   k. Three Light Traffic Signal[58]
4. Black elected officials throughout the south after the Civil War including US Representatives and a US Senator.

I need to point out that not all Progressives were totally Jim Crow. Though he believed in eugenics as a science, TR still promoted black people to government positions.

Other Republicans, Senator "Fighting Bob" LaFollette of Wisconsin and his wife Belle were at odds with President Wilson's segregationist policies. Fighting Bob believed that the past racism was the root cause of the nation's racial inequality. Lafollette and other progressive Republicans resisted Wilson's policy of disqualifying black people from aid to southern farmers.[59]

SAINT MARGARET, WEEDING THE HUMAN GARDEN

In July 2020 Planned Parenthood of Greater New York announced plans to remove Margaret Sanger's name from the Manhattan Health Center. PPGNY was also working with the city council, community board, city and the community to rename an honorary street sign that marks the "Margaret Sanger Square."[60]

"The removal of Margaret Sanger's name from our building is both a necessary and overdue step to reckon with our legacy and acknowledge Planned Parenthood's contributions to historical reproductive harm within communities of color," said the chair of PPGNY's board, Karen Seltzer. Seltzer continued. "Margaret Sanger's concerns and advocacy for reproductive health have been clearly documented, but so too has her racist legacy."

Sanger opened her first birth control clinic in Brooklyn in 1916.[61] At the time Brooklyn was where the "inferior races" from Europe lived, southern Europeans, Slavs, Latins and Jews, recent immigrants. For decades Margret Sangers apologists have detracted from Sangers true history.

On June 25, 1939, Sanger advanced a controversial "Negro Project," as she promoted birth control. In her autobiography she wrote about speaking to a Ku Klux Klan group and advocated for the eugenics approach to breeding for "the gradual suppression, elimination, and eventual extinction, of defective stocks–those 'human weeds' which threaten the blooming of the finest flowers of American civilization."

By the late 1930s with support from many eugenics' racists and Sanger's "Negro Advisory Council" she was able to establish clinics throughout the South. These clinics distributed contraceptives to the "reckless and irresponsible swarming and spawning...diseased elements of humanity."

The clinics also performed or promoted forced sterilizations. Sanger relied on support of the hand-picked black ministers, black doctors and state public health officials to promote the cause.[62]

Sanger wrote to DR. C.J. Gamble December 10th, 1939. In this letter she stated:

"The minister's work is also important and also, he should be trained, perhaps by the Federation as to our ideals and the goal that we hope to reach. We do not want the word to go out that we want to exterminate the Negro population and the minister is the man who can straighten out that idea if it ever occurs to any of their more rebellious members."[63]

Sanger's efforts were supported by some prominent black leaders such as W.E.B. DuBois, Mary McLeod

Bethune, and Rev. Adam Clayton Powell, Jr. These folks strongly supported the Progressive welfare reforms of the New Deal and the eugenics movement.[64]

When the Roe vs Wade decision legalized abortion in 1973 polling showed blacks were significantly less likely to support abortion. Today the abortion rate for black women is nearly 5 times that for the white population.[65]

During my time working in Baltimore, I was told numerous times, they (Republicans) had better not take away the right to an abortion. My understanding was that this position was in response to the conditions in the city, poverty, poor education and health care, crime, few opportunities.

Elvis Presley began to address "city-ghetto problems" in his 1969 hit "In the Ghetto."

As the snow flies,
on a cold and grey Chicago morn and
a poor little baby child is born in the ghetto.
And his momma cries.
Cause if there's one thing she don't need,
it's another hungry mouth to feed in the ghetto.......[66]

WHAT DID JESSE HAVE TO SAY

"What happens to the mind of a nation, that accepts the aborting of the life of a baby without a pang of conscience? What kind of a person, and what kind of a society will we have in 20 years hence if life can be taken so casually?" Jessie Jackson, (1977)[67]

"As a matter of conscience, I must oppose the use of federal funds for a policy of killing infants....in the abortion debate, one of the crucial questions is when does life begin. Anything growing is living. Therefore, human life begins when the sperm and egg join." Jesse Jackson, (1977)[68, 69]

By 1988 when he was running for US President Jackson said, "It is not right to impose private, religious and moral positions on public policy."[70] What happened? Jackson received money for his Presidential campaigns in 1988 from the proponents of eugenics.[71]

THE RAW NEW DEAL

Franklin Delano Roosevelt's, (FDR's) New Deal Reforms excluded non-whites from better economic opportunities. When social security was established in 1935, farm workers and domestics were excluded. These groups were predominantly non-white. Many unions excluded black people and Hispanics forced into low paying or dangerous jobs.[72]

FHA REDLINING

Prior to the 1930s banks making home loans typically required 50 percent down on a five-year note. In 1934 the government created the Federal Housing Administration to provide backing for loans the average Americans could afford. The new terms were typically the 10-20 percent down with 30 years financing that is common today. FHA underwriters established guidelines for lending and warned that the presence of one or two non-white families could undermine real estate values in the new suburbs. Government guidelines had been adopted by private industry. FDR's government institutionalized the national appraisal system where race was much a factor in real estate assessment as the condition of the property. All-white neighborhoods that were far away from minorities got green. The maps in the government guidelines red-lined minority neighborhoods. Between 1934 and 1962 the federal government underwrote 120 billion dollars in new home loans. As a result of the red lining practice less than two percent went to non-whites. Black GI's returning from WWII were denied access to federal housing and educational programs. This was presented in an educational documentary, "Race the Power of an Illusion" by the California Newsreel (2003).[73]

I first heard about red lining on a news broadcast in 1976. The report was talking about new legislation that had just been passed called the Community Reinvestment Act. The reporter explained that banks had established the red lines that had negatively impacted minority communities. A Republican politician, whose name I don't recall, was asked to comment, his answer puzzled me at the time. My recollection of his response is that "They are masters of creating a problem and then coming up with a solution to correct it."

The documentary, *Race the Power of an Illusion* did not mention the science of eugenics as a driving philosophy. As a documentary intended for educational purposes a more inclusive study would have been appropriate and more informative.

BALTIMORE, A CASE STUDY

The progression of segregation in Baltimore is covered in the book, *Not in My Neighborhood*[74] by Antero Pietila, a 35-year veteran reporter for the Baltimore Sun, in which he describes demographic change in the city of Baltimore. The following is an excerpt from the preface.

> Unlike New York, Chicago, Detroit, Boston, Philadelphia and Los Angeles, Baltimore is not usually a prominent part of the American urban narrative. It should be. In 1910 the city enacted the first law in American history that prohibited blacks from moving to white residential blocks and vice versa. When the US Supreme Court seven years later struck down the laws, Baltimore again became a model that other cities copied because private agreements had barred blacks and Jews from certain neighborhoods for years. Until the Supreme Court in 1948 declared them unenforceable, such restrictive covenants were the backbone of residential segregation throughout the nation. Baltimore was also a forerunner in blockbusting, large-scale, panic-induced racial turnover began during World War II, earlier by about a decade than in many other cities.
>
> Several chapters deal with blockbusting, a hot button issue after World War II when millions of whites fled America's city neighborhoods because they feared blacks.

Victims of their own hysteria, they sold their homes below market value to panic-peddling blockbusters, who then flipped them to blacks at extraordinary markups. The book reveals a previously overlooked initial motivation of blockbusting—transferring the astronomical modernization liabilities of substandard housing to unsuspecting black buyers."[75]

Pietila documented that:

"Two diametrically opposed responses to blockbusting emerged: whites saw enemies who enable a black invasion; blacks acknowledged blockbusters as profiteers' but also welcomed them as agents of liberating desegregation. This fundamental disagreement split the Baltimore fair-housing advocates. They were further weakened by mutual mistrust: black leaders were suspicious of Jews; Jewish leaders did not trust blacks."[76]

Additionally:

"Blockbusters also were not a monolith. A central figure in this narrative is an African American blockbuster who saw the breaking of white neighborhoods as his civil rights mission similar to restaurant sit-ins in which he was repeatedly arrested."[77]

The problems for black people in Maryland were the result of both parties. Over time Baltimoreans migrated from the city to Baltimore County, which surrounds Baltimore. The book documents how the county contained blacks through zoning and other actions. Several county executives were exposed for extorsion during their time in office. County Executive Dale Anderson, Democrat went to prison for extorting bribes and not reporting them as income. The bribes were for zoning approvals and favors. The investigation into Anderson exposed similar corruption by his predecessor Spiro T Agnew, Republican who was at that point President Richard Nixon's Vice President. Agnew was forced to resign.[78]

As a society we are struggling with the result of the discrimination implemented by federal, state, and local governments. Over the last 100+ years most of the policies were developed by college educated persons and sometimes in the institutions themselves. During the 1960s this nation passed the Great Society programs providing support for those who previously had been deprived through programs set up by earlier "intellectual elites." I don't think these programs have worked as advertised. Since that time, the system has been overhauled numerous times and yet no improvement.

"No government ever voluntarily reduces itself in size. Government programs, once launched, never disappear. Actually, a government bureau is the nearest thing to eternal life we'll ever see on this earth." Ronald Reagan[79]

I was fortunate to have never been laid off over a 45-year career. I rode through many downturns and saw others pushed out the door. I was a white-collar employee of a government contractor. During that time, I watched as factories all over the country were shut down and blue- collar and white-collar jobs were shipped overseas. Globalization, promoted by societies elites, has hollowed out communities though out this nation. Our cities have largely become "opportunity deserts" where the jobs black men used to work to support their families no longer exist. I eventually realized most politicians didn't seem to care. It's as if the politicians wanted to keep the poor dependent on them to ensure their vote. Now I realize they were getting wealthy through bribes and corruption. Politicians getting wealthy while they made the system work for their wealthy donors domestic and foreign. Our fellow citizens in our cities need jobs and opportunities rather than continued dependence. Is welfare a trap set by the elites to ensure a constant population of poor needy people they can continuously advocate for? After all, if the government solved poverty what would those government employees do?

"One of the problems in dealing with programs for blacks is that vast empires can be built on these programs. These programs prevent poverty among bureaucrats, economists, statisticians and others" (Thomas Sowell, 1980 Fairmont Conference).[80, 81]

A hundred years ago, educated elites were promoting the idea we needed experts to plan society. What did we get? A resegregated government, "separate but equal education" with Plessy vs Fergusson, eugenics/scientific racism, redlining, minority exclusion from early social security and the GI bill. What are the educated elites delivering today? We can see the results in America's cities and it's not a pretty sight. Students trapped in failed schools simply because of the zip code they live in, broken homes, extreme violence, drugs, abandoned decaying homes and buildings. But we know the politicians care because they tell us so. Will they ever apologize?

When I was volunteering in Baltimore residents told me if I wanted to understand the situation watch the HBO program "The Wire." If you want to see how warring drug gangs rule the streets and schools, tune in. I was told the schools fail the serious students because gang members who don't care about education are a constant disruption. This series was written by a former investigative reporter for the Baltimore Sun, David Simon.[82]

I binge watched the program completing all five seasons in a few weeks. What "The Wire" depicts is the result of government policies since the Great Society programs of the 1960s. But it's not just Baltimore, similar conditions are present in New York, Philadelphia, Cleveland, Detroit, Chicago, Milwaukee, Minneapolis, and on and on. America's cities have long been killing zones for our black population. It's as though they've found a new way to implement the policies of societal improvement from the first half of the 1900's.

"Despite the grand myth that black economic progress began with the passage of the civil rights laws, the cold fact is that the poverty rate among black people fell from

87 percent in 1940 to 47 percent by 1960. This was before any of those programs began."

"Nearly a hundred years after the supposed 'legacy of slavery' found most black children (78 percent) being raised in two-parent families in 1960; but thirty years after the liberal welfare state found the great majority of black children being raised by a single parent."

Thomas Sowell[83, 84]

In these comments, Thomas Sowell is referring to conditions in the mid 1980s. I suspect the issue is much worse today. My greatest experience working with Habitat for Humanity was attending a dedication ceremony where the home was turned over to the new owner. The event occurred right before Christmas around 2012. Rather than the yellow ribbon they normally use for the ceremony a red ribbon was hung on the door. The woman taking owner- ship of that home was a first-time homeowner about my own age. Her church was there to celebrate with prayers, singing, and a message of thanks. She was moving in with her elderly mother and seven grandchildren. The interme- diate generation, the parents of her grandchildren, were not on the scene. I did not ask and did not have any insight as to why, just conditions in the city.

There is another Baltimore experience I wanted to share, one that shook me. A member of my church and I had bought flowers to plant in a vacant lot across from the church. It was an effort to beautify the neighborhood. The youth of the church, particularly the very young children, ages 2 to 8, came out to help. We split into two teams then began instructing these young children on how to plant and care for the flowers.

When we were almost finished a small boy of about three came over and gave me a hug. I stood up and then he asked me a question which I couldn't understand. I bent over to listen, and he asked if he could come home with me. The thought brings tears to my eyes as I am writing. I mentioned this to his grandmother. Her response was that he has no male role models to look up to. I have heard many conservative commentators state that father absence is the biggest problem in the black community. I have also been told that young men in the cities seek the gang life for substitute male role models. It is my belief the multitude of government programs is the cause of the problems in our cities today. Government is one institution in our society which isn't governed by the laws of economics. If one government program fails, there is always more money to spent on another. Private industry would go broke with this business model.

"Welfare's purpose should be to eliminate, as far as possible, the need for its own existence," stated Ronald Reagan.[85] That is if the program is working for the targeted recipient not the administrators and politicians.

To paraphrase what Morpheus said:

The blue pill will erase these historical facts as if you had never heard them, you will have no awareness...With the blue pill you can go back to your ordinary life working in an ordinary cubicle and live the status quo like everyone else has for generations. Just accept what our Progressive overlords have told us for decades was true.

The red pill, however, is another story. The red pill will open your eyes to live fully in reality. with better understanding of the evils from the Jim Crow Progressive Common Era forward. Strive hard to understand the matrix/Deep State which is keeping Western Civilization unknowingly in a deep sleep and disillusionment. Take the red pill you will wake up and get control of his life for the first time ever; knowing that American Jim Crow Progressives preceded the Nazi's in the development of scientific White Supremacy. Will you take the red pill? Join me in traveling further down the rabbit hole to a world with eyes opening wider.

CHAPTER 5
CRIMINAL JUSTICE REFORM

Criminal justice in the United States has changed much from the revolutionary era to today. I do not want to rehash the old-time justice. As a nation we no longer put people in stocks, tie convicts to a pole and lash them, and we no longer use the hangman's gallows. Instead, I would like to reflect on more recent developments.

As a young man during the '70s I was aware that Republicans were more the law-and-order party and Democrats the softer on crime, the more "compassionate" party. That made sense to me as the Democrats ran the cities where higher crime rates occurred. I rationalized that Democrats were taking it easy on their constituents. I didn't really think about why there was more crime in the cities, just knew that it was that way.

Throughout the '70s and '80s crime in our cities continued to increase. In an attempt to protect the public, the US Congress took action. The 1984 Comprehensive Crime Control Act eliminated parole in the federal system and established mandatory minimum-sentencing guidelines.[1]

This bill was eventually incorporated into an appropriations bill that passed with a vote of 78–11 in the Senate and 252–60 in the House. There were twenty-one co-sponsors in the Senate. However, this legislation did not resolve the crime issue.

Crime became the topic of discussion again in the 1990s. There were calls for the government to address crime by ministers, politicians, and leaders of the black community. There was a demand for safer streets. The Violent Crime Control and Law Enforcement Act of 1994 had been referred to as the "Clinton Crime Bill" as President Clinton sign the bill into law and Hillary Clinton was a major proponent. At the time this legislation was being promoted I was surprised at the commentary being used. My recollection was that Hillary Clinton used rhetoric like "super predators" who had "no conscience, no empathy" and who need to be brought "to heel." These words shocked me as it was clear that would be extremely hard on the minority communities they were advocating for.

PRESIDENT CLINTON CALLS FOR THREE STRIKE RULE

President Clinton urged Congress saying:

"First, we must recognize that most violent crimes are committed by a small percentage of criminals who too often break the laws even when they are on parole. Now those who commit crimes should be punished. And those who commit repeated violent crimes should be told, when you commit a third violent crime, you will be put away, and put away for good; three strikes and you are out." [2]

The bill also included significant funding for hiring 100,000 police officers and build prisons to house the newly incarcerated.

THE AUTHOR-JOE BIDEN

During the 2020 primaries I was dumbfounded to learn that candidate, Joseph Biden had been the author, in the Senate, of that 1994 crime bill. In 1994 the media had given so much attention to First Lady Hillary Clinton, that I wasn't aware the author was, Senator Biden. The media has a tremendous ability to frame the narrative.

In 1993 during negotiations, Senator Biden stated:

"Take back the streets. It doesn't matter whether or not the person that is accosting your son or daughter, or my son or daughter, my wife, your husband, my mother, your parents it doesn't matter whether or not they were deprived as a youth. It doesn't matter whether or not they had no background to enable them to become socialized in the fabric of society. It doesn't matter whether or not they are the victims of society. The end result is they are about to knock my mother on the head with a lead pipe, shoot my sister, beat up my wife, take on my sons. So, I want to ask what made them do this. They must be taken off the street, that's number one. There's a consensus on that. Unless we do something about the cadre of young people. Tens of thousands of them, born out of wedlock, without parents, without supervision, without any structure, without any conscience developing because they literally, I yield myself three more minutes, because they literally have not been socialized. They literally have not had an opportunity; we should focus on them now. If we don't, they will or, a portion of them will, become the predators 15 years from now. And Madam president we have predators on our streets, that society has in fact in part because of its neglect, created. Again, it does not mean because we created them that we somehow forgive them or do not take them out of society to protect my family and yours from them. They are beyond the pale many of those people, beyond the pale. And it's a sad commentary on society. We have no choice but to take them out of society. And the truth is, we don't know very well how to rehabilitate them at that point, that's the sad truth. I'm the guy that said rehabilitation, when it occurs, we don't understand it and notice it and when we even notice it and when it occurs, we don't know why. So you cannot make rehabilitation a condition for release. That's why in our system the federal system you serve 85 percent of your time. It's a shame but we don't know how to rehabilitate but there is a consensus, and I will cease.

We must make the streets safer. I don't care why someone is a malefactor in society. I don't care why someone is antisocial. I don't care why they've become a sociopath. We have an obligation to cordon them off from the rest of society. Try to help them, try to change the behavior. That's what we do in this bill we have drug treatment and we have other treatments to try and deal with it but they are in jail. Away from my mother, your husband, our families. But we would be absolutely stupid as a society if we didn't recognize the condition that nurture those folks still exist and we must deal with that."[3]

The House vote resulted in Democrats providing 80 percent of the yea votes, Republicans 67 percent of the nay votes.[4] In the Senate Democrats provided 90 percent of the yea votes, Republicans 95 percent of the nay votes,[5] with dominant support from the Democrat party the bill passed and was signed into law September 13th 1994 by President William Jefferson Clinton.[6] Over approximately the next six years the Clinton administration oversaw the implementation of the crime bill and the building of the prison industrial complex.

On Friday February 10, 2023, Real Time with Bill Maher and Overtime on HBO, Bill Maher's guests were Democratic strategist Paul Begala, pollster Kristen Soltis Anderson, and counter terrorism expert Malcom Nance. The following was part of the panel discussion.

Paul Begala:

"Democrats and my fellow liberals, it's the people we supposedly care about who are the victims of crime. It's those folks who are voting for more security, more safety, more and better cops and it's the white liberals who want to defund the police."

Bill Maher: "This is a big Achilles heel for Democrats, is it not?"
Paul Begala:

"Oh, they need to get out in front of it, I want a Democrat to stand up and say some people belong in jail. You know the rapists, the murderers.... "

[Audience: 1 clap, then a few more join]
Bill Maher:

"One clap for that...I think that's interesting; I'm going to go out on a limb, some people do belong in jail."

The panel also discussed how it's poor kids who were hurt most by school shutdowns.[7]
Does Paul Begala have a poor memory? Does he not know that President Clinton already signed Criminal Justice Reform in 1994? I would point out this dialogue was edited out when the show posted it on YouTube.[8]
I believe that is why the Democrat Party was so upset with Donald Trump in 2016 when he spoke to the black community.

"Look how much African American communities have suffered under Democratic control. To those I say the following, what do you have to lose by trying something new like Trump? What do you have to lose? What do you have to lose? I say it again What do you have to lose? You're living in poverty; your schools are no good. You have no jobs. 58 percent of your youth is unemployed. What the hell do you have to lose? America must reject the bigotry of Hillary Clinton who sees communities of color only as votes not as human beings worthy of a better future."[9]

A CALL FOR CHANGE

If we are going to remove statues placed by past Democrats, then why during the 2020 election promote the author of the legislative disaster in question? This 1994 Crime Bill worked as it was written, and no one can say "we're sorry." They just blame the police. In the seventies and eighties, we were told the problems in the cities were because of racist white officers. I'm sure there was some of that. We were told we need more officers that look like the communities they patrol. Now we have many minority officers the new narrative is that it's a racist system. Occasionally we hear the term "death by cop" which is described as "an incident in which suicidal individuals provoke law enforcement officers to shoot them."[10]

I've never heard a comparable term "death by criminal" in which an officer leaves for work with a death wish hoping to be killed in the line of duty. Does it exist? High homicide rates have existed in America's cities for decades mostly driven by gang-on-gang and black-on- black violence. By ignoring this fact, the politicians aren't addressing the root causes or those policies that resulted in high crime in the first place. It's easy to understand why the poor in Americas cities accept the statement there's "systemic racism," they are living it. For generations conditions have been getting worse. But the problems are the result of elitist government policies from the Jim Crow Progressive Common Era to today. Unfortunately, the academics, bureaucrats and politicians responsible blame others and distract from their or institutional culpability. They need to keep the public divided to perpetuate their positions.   Let me remind you of the summation from chapter 4; "they are masters of creating a problem and then coming up with a solution to correct it."

The last twenty-five years have proven Senator Biden to be correct, the government doesn't know how to fix the problems. In fact, the government has only made the problems worse. As Thomas Sowell stated, "It is hard to imagine a more stupid or more dangerous way of making decisions than by putting those decisions in the hands of people who pay no price for being wrong."[11]

President Reagan during his first inaugural speech commented, "In this present crisis government is not the answer to our problems; government is the problem."[12]

President Reagan was referring to the economic problems brought by federal spending, deficits, excessive taxation, and other federal budget issues, but it applies here as well. Has Senator Biden's 1994 legislation proven Reagan was right?

It is a mistake not to search out root causes. However, there are many and I suspect the solutions put forward are seldom comprehensive or effective. People have told me that there are racists in our society. I don't doubt that there are, however, the individual racist is limited to the amount of damage he or she can do. A government program on the other hand, has the force of law and government agencies to enforce those policies. We discussed segregation and redlining earlier. Even well intended policies that fail yet obtain "eternal life" through the inertia of government can have the same devastating impact. America's longest war, the war on poverty began 60 years ago yet poverty is on the increase. I'll speak to this in chapter twelve. We've been discussing education reform for generations now yet educational attainment continues to decline. However, the educational infrastructure has continued to increase at all levels of government.

During my time volunteering in Baltimore, conversing with residents, I realized they made decisions very differently than I anticipated. One observation was there was no long-term planning. It did not take long to sort this out. Given a lack of financial resources or educational opportunity it's difficult to plan for the future. Another was the extreme concern over abortion rights. The despair was palpable, if your tossed by the storms of life what do you have control of. As it turns out Margret Sangers Planned Parenthood is generally located very conveniently in most cities. As Elvis sang in 1968: "Cause if there's one thing she don't need, it's another hungry mouth to

feed in the ghetto. . ." I struggled intellectually and emotionally with this reality. But my goal was to understand
not to judge. From my perspective their decisions did not
serve them well in the long term. In his book "Discovering
City Ministry Secrets" Doug Koenigsberg presented two
terms which helped clear up my confusion, "survivalist"
and "intentionalist."[13]

I am an intentionalist, which is a person who sets
goals and plans for their life then implements those plans.
I learned early that by planning and hard work I could
achieve goals. By mowing lawns in my neighborhood as a
youth, I was able to save money for a new bike from Sears
and Roebuck. After high school and college graduation I
embarked on a forty-three-year career and never missed
a paycheck. During the economic turmoil of the 1990's and
again with the 2008 recession I made career changes on
my terms, never by layoff. Now comfortably retired, I'm
living in a fine home with my wonderful wife of 40+ years.
Along the way we were able to provide a stable yet sometimes chaotic environment to raise our two children. And
now I get to watch my children chart their own paths in
life. I also have time and resources to pursue my interests,
travel, gardening, writing this book and soon woodwork-
ing. My intentionality served me well for decades.

The folks I observed in Baltimore are survivalists; that
is they have limited education and resources to implement a plan and are often simply reacting to what the day
throws at them in order to survive. They learn to react
instinctively to the actions of others on the street. They

may dream of escaping the situation in Baltimore but not for long. Those who wish to graduate high school and get out of the situation are trapped in a failing school system simply because of the zip code they live in. They must deal with the reality of the moment and are never able to plan their future as I did.

Over 100 years ago this nation embarked in the direction of the educated elite planning our society. There have been positive developments but as pointed out in chapter 3, there were serious negative results which are clearly visible in our cities today. For several decades after the 1994 Crime Bill the accused would be overcharged and forced to plea bargain. As a result, many people with low level non-violent offenses that may have been overlooked in the past now have a criminal record. I suspect most of these folks were survivalist, just trying to get through the day. Making their way in communities that are educational and opportunity deserts.

A NEW STEP FORWARD.

President Trump was anxious to sign the bipartisan First Step Act into law on Dec. 21, 2018. During his 2019 State of the Union address, President Trump proudly described the law saying: "This legislation reformed sentencing laws that have wrongly and disproportionately harmed the African-American community."

President Trump further explained: "The First Step Act gives nonviolent offenders the chance to reenter society as productive, law-abiding citizens. Now, states across the country are following our lead. America is a nation that believes in redemption."[14]

As reported by Fox News:

> The First Step Act—or the Formerly Incarcerated Reenter Society Transformed Safely Transitioning Every Person Act—is, at its core, a directive for the Justice Department to establish a system to assess the risk of a person to re-offend as well as to create housing or other incentives for offenders to participate in recidivism reduction programs.
>
> The bill, which passed the Senate 87-12, culminates years of negotiations and gave the Trump administration a signature policy victory. It's been heralded by conservatives and liberals, celebrities and Jared Kushner, the president's son-in-law, who worked the halls of Congress for months to forge a compromise.[15]

President Trump was proud that his economic policies had reduced unemployment in minority communities to the lowest levels in recorded times. The opportunities and job openings were so great that many employers began hiring convicted felons which they would not have done in the past. In my opinion having a good job opportunity is an excellent way to avoid recidivism.

But to adequately help people following a life of crime we need to change the educational system. We need a change that is intended to serve the students and not the teachers' unions or a political party. To end the school-to-prison pipeline, change is required. It is finally time for school choice, where the money follows a student rather than trapping them in a failed school simply because of the zip code they live in.

Since the First Step Act, many Democrat states and municipalities took a different tact on crime. The Democrat party returned to soft on crime policies, opening the jails and releasing many violent offenders. In addition, many prosecutors, district attorneys, et cetera, stopped enforcing laws that were on the books. Some states have implemented cashless bail which results in many violent offenders being released before the arresting officers can finish the paperwork. As a result of this Democrat party criminal justice reform, crime has spiked all over the country and citizens live in fear. Minority communities were most affected by violence. However, crime spilled over into more affluent communities as well. And so, it's time for a new round of criminal justice reform. Are the twists and turns in Democrat policies an effort to avoid responsibility for the impact of the 1994 bill? Stop and think about that.

CNN reported that due to the increase in shop lifting, Target will be closing nine stores in the fall of 2023. These stores include the East Harlem NY, two in Seattle, three in Portland, and three locations in San Francisco and Oakland CA. CNN went on to state:

"Target is closing stores in cities that underwent significant initiatives...they pointed out there was a substantial increase in retail theft because once you take jail out of the equation as a possibility from the legal process people think it's just like shopping without money. So, it's less of a deterrent essential. Much less of a deterrent cause if you look at New York City, we have 300 people who are responsible for 30 percent of the all the shop lifting and they have over 4000 arrests between them and 70 percent of them are not in jail, this is their job."[16]

Target released a statement stating:

"We cannot continue operating these stores because theft and organized retail crime are threatening the safety of our team and guests and contributing to unsustainable business performance...We know that our stores serve an important role in their communities, but we can only be successful if the working and shopping environment is safe for all."[17]

CNN reported that it's not just big box stores but small business being affected as well.

In addition to shoplifting, violent crime is up dramatically.

CHAPTER 6
NATIONAL ANTHEM

OH SAY CAN YOU HANDLE THE TRUTH?

When my son was in grade school, I became a leader in the Cub Scout pack at his school. In addition to serving as committee chair, I gladly took on a position that in my day would have been called the "den mother." Cub Scouts is an adult led program with many parents volunteering.

The boys enjoyed many weekend field trips to various facilities in Maryland where we live. One such trip was to Fort McHenry and I was excited to be at that historic spot.

I enjoyed watching the Rangers explaining the Battle of Fort McHenry to these young boys. I suspect the members of our den who are now young men remember climbing the walls of the fort and helping fold the big flag. While standing in the fort, I was thinking, it was here that Americans withstood the bombardment, and out there in the bay Francis Scott Key wrote the now famous words.

CHAPTER 6: NATIONAL ANTHEM

As a patriotic American, I've always been proud to sing the national anthem prior to a sporting event. Until recently, I didn't realize there was more than one verse. When the recent controversy over the national anthem started in 2016, I was surprised to learn otherwise.

BATTLE OF JOURNALISTS

In researching this chapter on the national anthem, I've looked at numerous references but will contrast comments from two politically divergent sources. One source is an August 2017 article by Jefferson Morley in the far-left publication "Salon." The second source is an October 2016 article by Steve Bias in the far-right publication, "The New American." Let's continue down the rabbit hole.

As Steve Bias reported:

"When San Francisco 49ers quarterback Colin Kaepernick opted to figuratively "stand up" against alleged oppression of black people in America by not standing for the playing of the national anthem in a pre-season game of the National Football League (NFL), it vividly illustrated the cultural divisions that exist in American society.

"I am not going to stand up to show pride in a flag for a country that oppresses black people," the second-string pro player said, in explaining his action after his initial pre-season game protest. Kaepernick's sit-down protest has continued into the regular season."

Bias went on to report protests at several high schools around the country, most notably Woodrow Wilson High School in Camden, New Jersey where:

"Coach Preston Brown and his assistants even took a knee along with their high-school players. The district issued a statement indicating that, while they support "standing for the flag," it is a "personal issue, and we strongly respect our students' experiences and their exercising our country's First Amendment rights."

In fact, while the controversy has centered on the playing of "The Star-Spangled Banner," it has been somewhat overlooked that Kaepernick's problem is really with the entire country. Kaepernick was alluding to incidents in which black criminal suspects have been shot by police officers—particularly white officers—such as the situation in Ferguson, Missouri, where a white officer had shot a young black man who was allegedly surrendering with his arms up in the air while pleading, "Don't shoot!"—giving birth to the "Hands up, don't shoot!" mantra used in protests after the event. A grand jury refused to indict the white officer when multiple witnesses—almost all AfricanAmerican—and forensic evidence disputed that claim, as did a US Justice Department report.

The reality is that 93 percent of black homicide victims are murdered by other blacks, and most of the rest are killed by Hispanics. The vast majority of people shot by police are white, and whites are actually more likely to be shot by law-enforcement officers. Police killings of

CHAPTER 6: NATIONAL ANTHEM

black suspects have actually declined dramatically over the past few decades."[1]

The irony is that students at Woodrow Wilson High School were protesting the anthem which will become clearer later in the chapter. I believe the whole anthem protest, removing statues, and charges of systemic racism are to deflect from the realities of inner-city crime and failing schools which city and party leadership have no answer for. The citizens of America's inner cities are victims of the policies which resulted in those conditions.

Jefferson Morley's article began with:

"Confederate war memorials are just the beginning. The removal of a statue of Chief Justice Roger Taney from its pride of place in the capital of Maryland is the manifestation of a popular awakening that goes beyond bringing down statues of Confederate heroes like Stonewall Jackson."

What we are seeing is the popular repudiation–and violent defense–of the neo-Confederate ideology that has shaped the symbols of American public life for the last 150 years. Some of these symbols now draw protests, while others are woven into public life.

For example, observing Memorial Day and singing "The Star-Spangled Banner" are uncontroversial patriotic gestures, yet there is no disputing that neo-Confederates developed these rituals. That doesn't necessarily mean the holiday and the national anthem should be jettisoned, along with Robert. E. Lee statues, only that their historical roots should be recognized and taught.

The dethroning of Taney shows why. Taney, who wrote the Supreme Court's 1857 Dred Scott decision that effectively legalized slavery nationwide, was never a Confederate. He owned people as property, and defended slavery, but he never advocated rebellion. After the Civil War began, Taney continued to serve the US government as Chief Justice until his death in 1864.

Yet his statue had to go, said Gov. Lawrence Hogan, a Republican. In his statement ordering the removal, Hogan declared: "While we cannot hide from our past—nor should we—the time has come to make clear the difference between properly acknowledging our past and glorifying the darkest chapters of our history."[2]

Governor Hogan's intent is correct. However, I would suggest a rephasing: For too long our institutions abused their responsibility and privilege to hide their culpability in the darkest chapters of our history. The time has come to expose the truth for a more inclusive, robust under-standing of our history by We the People. Were the statues placed in an attempt to heal the sectional divisions, north and south still present at the time? The truth is that those statues were once a source of pride for the Democrat party; could it be the Ivy League as well?

In addressing the phrase considered most offen-sive, Bias wrote: "Did Francis Scott Key, the author of "The Star-Spangled Banner" (originally a poem entitled

"Defence of Fort McHenry"), write the song to be a racist anthem, or otherwise promote social injustice? Shaun King of the New York Daily News made that charge, asserting that in the third stanza, Key "openly celebrates" the killing of slaves. In fact, King insists that Key's stirring tune "was rooted in the celebration of slavery and the murder of Africans in America." The lyrics King refers to are: "No refuge could save the hireling and slave from the terror of flight, or the gloom of the grave." According to King, black men–called the Corps of Colonial Marines–were serving in the British military. "Key despised them. He was glad to see them experience terror and death in war—to the point that he wrote a poem about it."

This is deceitful. The song certainly does not "celebrate" slavery nor the murder of slaves. It is likely that Key did despise anyone who was involved in the attack upon Baltimore's Fort McHenry during the War of 1812, which inspired the writing of the poem which later became our national anthem. One might recall that Americans were also not too fond of the German mercenaries, the Hessians, whom King George hired to suppress the American War for Independence.

Attempting to invade a country, after all, whether one is German or African, is not the best way to win the love of that country.

Key's own record on slavery was certainly mixed. Although he did own slaves, he also freed slaves. As a lawyer, Key took on cases of several slaves seeking their liberation–cases for which he took no fee. His frequent

public criticisms of slavery's worst cruelties were so powerful that they were noted in a newspaper account of his
death. The writer stated, "Key convinced me that slavery
was wrong—radically wrong."

One of Key's most famous cases of legal work was
for his friend Congressman John Randolph of Roanoke.
After Randolph's death in 1833, Key and other attorneys
worked to carry out his wishes that his more than 400
slaves would be not only be freed but provided with funds
from Randolph's estate to buy them land in the free state
of Ohio so that they could support themselves. Hardly the
resumé of a pro-slavery fanatic, as he is unfairly pictured
by King.[3]

The John Randolph mentioned here is the third
Virginian mentioned previously. Francis Scott Key was
one of the lawyers working to enact John Randolph's will.

During the colonial period King George denied several
colonies the authority to end slavery within their own colony. After the Revolution had begun King George offered
the slaves freedom if they fought for the Crown, not as
though this move made him virtuous. The United States
declared war on Great Britain in 1812 because they were
impressing American sailors, black and white, into service in the British Navy. The reason the hirelings are in
the third verse is likely that they participated in the failed
British ground assault on Baltimore the day before.

Morely's contribution to understanding this history is
included below.[4]

Likewise, Key's "Star-Spangled Banner," with its

lyrics deriding black people who took up arms to gain their freedom in the War of 1812, became a point of pride for Southerners. In the decades following the Civil War, the defeated South strove to establish rituals such as Memorial Day, which honored the veterans of northern and southern armies equally, implying equality of respect for their causes.

Honoring "The Star-Spangled Banner" was another such ritual. In 1914, on the centennial of Key's writing the song, supporters launched a campaign to designate "The Star-Spangled Banner" as the one and only national anthem. At the time "The Battle Hymn of the Republic" and "America the Beautiful" were also considered national anthems, especially in the northern states. The campaign to elevate the "Banner" was, as one Boston magazine noted in 1914, "a sectarian movement." That sect was the white supremacist South.

BATTLE OVER THE BANNER

Long before Colin Kaepernick had the best-selling jersey in the National Football League, "The Star-Spangled Banner" was the cause of an American culture war. In the 1920s pacifists, liberals, and African Americans resisted elevating Key's stirring song because they objected to its militaristic and racist overtones. Confederate sympathizers responded by taking their cause to Congress.

In the 1920s, as blacks and white liberals denounced Jim Crow laws and lynchings, the campaign for "The

Star-Spangled Banner" became a way to wrap the ideology of the Confederacy in the red, white, and blue bunting of American patriotism.

African Americans were especially resistant to the appeal of "Oh say can you see?"

In 1927, poet James Weldon Johnson and his brother Rosamund composed a song to commemorate the birthday of Abraham Lincoln called "Lift Every Voice and Sing." The song's popularity among people of color made it known as the "Negro National Anthem." Johnson, also an NAACP activist, denied there was anything in his song to conflict with "The Star-Spangled Banner." But he couldn't resist adding that the "Banner" was "difficult to sing," and that "its sentiments are boastful and bloodthirsty."

The national anthem culture war of the 1920s pitted the emancipationist values of the North against the white supremacist credo of the South.

The Southerners won the war in March 1931. That's when President Herbert Hoover signed a law, sponsored by Maryland Congressman John Linthicum, formally designating "The Star-Spangled Banner" as the national anthem.

OH, SAY CAN YOU SEE?

The neo-Confederate spirit animating those who wanted Americans to sing Key's song after every public event was obvious. They marched under the Confederate flag. Contemporary newspaper reports tell the story.

On June 14, 1931, the National Society of the Daughters of 1812 and the state of Maryland sponsored a ceremony at War Memorial Plaza in Baltimore to celebrate the new national anthem. The parade was led by a column of Boy Scouts carrying three flags: the Stars and Stripes, the red and gold flag of Maryland, and the Stars and Bars of the army of the Confederate States of America.

Marching in the parade were the very old men who had fought in 1861. The 22-year-old Union men who fought at Gettysburg in 1863 were now 90 years old. These dogged veterans of the Grand Army of the Republic (GAR) were stunned to find themselves falling in behind the banner of their former enemies. They pulled up short.

The story made the news: "GAR Balks at Southern Flag in Parade," reported the Baltimore Sun. General John F. King, past national commander of the GAR, "ordered the Union men to disband and fall out of line," said the Baltimore Afro-America.

A CONFEDERATE "BANNER?"

Those who wanted "The Star-Spangled Banner" to serve as the national anthem could not have been more explicit in their politics.

Ella Holloway, the leader of the pro "banner" forces for more than two decades, defended the flying of the Confederate flag as patriotic and dismissed the walkout of the Union veterans.

"It is shame to spoil such a beautiful occasion with

talk of friction," she wrote in a letter to the Sun. "There is no North. There is no South. Nor East nor West. We are a 'sovereign nation of many sovereign states, one and inseparable. A perfect Union.'"

The Confederate flag, she declared, was also a star-spangled banner.

"The Stars and Stripes, our country's flag," she went on, "escorted the 'stars and bars' of the slaveholding states in the pageant of June 14, proclaiming to all the world our loyalty to it and all it stands for."

In short, neo-Confederates elevated "The Star-Spangled Banner" from patriotic tune to national anthem as a way of honoring southern slaveowners' rebellion."[5]

The details presented by Morley are fascinating and an important insight into the times. I personally had not heard of "Lift Every Voice and Sing" until about 2010. What a beautiful composition. James Weldon Johnson was not only a prolific writer of text and song, he was also one of the Black Republicans appointed by President Theodore Roosevelt to government positions. Johnson served as United States consul at Puerto Cabello, Venezuela, from 1906 to 1908, and then in Nicaragua. Johnson was in government service through the Taft administration. I have not found any records indicating why he left the government.[6, 7, 8]

Did he leave voluntarily or was he forced out as Wilson re-segregated the federal government, under Jim Crow Progressivism? After leaving government service Johnson became a powerful advocate for civil rights. Were "Lift

Every Voice and Sing" and possibly the Juneteenth celebration, buried by Jim Crow Progressives, and only now resurfacing in the general public as a political convenience? I would point out that Morley stated that "In the 1920s, as blacks and white liberals denounced Jim Crow laws and lynchings..." I would add, I've seen different dates regarding when this song was first shared with the public. I suspect 1901 is the correct date.[9]

Definition of Liberal: "Having, expressing, or following views or policies that favor the freedom of individuals to act or express themselves in a manner of their own choosing."[10]

The Jim Crow Progressive Movement of the late 1800s and early 1900s was not liberal, it was authoritarian, working to improve the nation by aiding those they believed to be superior individuals, white people. This is where white privilege began. Progressives hid the fact they had laid the groundwork science used by Hitler's Germany, the Nazis. Today's progressives in academia and elsewhere are weaponizing our nations institutions against any resistance to once again divide "We the People" and mold society to fit their "intellectual" fantasies.

AND NOW—THE REST OF THE STORY

Francis Scott Key describing the Battle of Baltimore wrote, "It seemed as though mother earth had opened and was vomiting shot and shell in a sheet of fire and brimstone,"[11] Fort McHenry was under bombardment for 25 hours.

As the sun rose the morning of September 14, 1814, Key could see the large American flag waving over the fort. He began writing "The Star-Spangled Banner" on the back of a letter and completed the first verse. The remaining three verses were complete after returning to Baltimore.

Originally titled: "Defence of Fort McHenry" a local printer first published the song, then two Baltimore newspapers. It soon spread along the east coast and by November of that year was titled "The Star-Spangled Banner." "Yankee Doodle" and "Hail, Columbia" remained more popular than the "Banner" among Patriotic songs during the early 1800s, however, with the Civil War and Lincoln's assassination, the "Banner" and the American flag gained a deeper meaning as symbols of national unity.[12]

John Charles Linthicum was a scholarly man who studied history at Johns Hopkins about the same time as Woodrow Wilson. His first wife Eugenia May Biden, died early in 1897. Could she have been a distant relative of the current President whose father was born in Baltimore?[13]

Linthicum's second wife was a promoter of the "Banner" as a national anthem and friend of Mrs. Reuben Ross (Ella) Holloway, mentioned previously.[14] However, the US Military had adopted the "Banner" for ceremonial purposes by the later 1890's. President Woodrow Wilson designated the "Banner" as the national anthem in 1916 via executive order.[15] In 1918 Linthicum submitted a bill to the House to officially make "The Star-Spangled Banner" the national anthem. The legislation was not adopted until 1931, and President Hoover signed the bill.[16]

Could it be Republicans TR and Fighting Bob Lafollette were some of those holding out for "The Battle Hymn of the Republic"? It was about the same time President Wilsons issued an executive order making the "Banner" the national anthem. So, is Woodrow Wilson the chief neo-Confederate to elevate "The Star-Spangled Banner" from patriotic tune to national anthem as a way of honoring southern slaveowners' rebellion, the "Lost Cause"?

LIFT EVERY VOICE AND SING

Sunday February 12, 2023, the NFL had Sheryl Lee Ralph perform "Lift Every Voice and Sing" before the national anthem.[17] This song/hymn was written to commemorate Abraham Lincoln's birthday.[18] The Star-Spangled Banner was promoted during the Jim Crow Progressive common era to promote, in my opinion, white unity in both north and south. But that history has been hidden for some time, not by the common citizen, but by elitists abusing their positions in society.

How did this "Lift Every Voice and Sing" spread? I think it best to read the words of the poet himself.

"A group of young men in Jacksonville, Florida, arranged to celebrate Lincoln's birthday in 1900. My brother, J. Rosamond Johnson, and I decided to write a song to be sung at the exercises. I wrote the words, and he wrote the music. Our New York publisher, Edward B. Marks, made mimeographed copies for us, and the song was taught to and sung by a chorus of five hundred colored school children.

Shortly afterwards my brother and I moved away from Jacksonville to New York, and the song passed out of our minds. But the school children of Jacksonville kept singing it; they went off to other schools and sang it; they became teachers and taught it to other children. Within twenty years it was being sung over the South and in some other parts of the country. Today the song, popularly known as the Negro National Hymn, is quite generally used.

The lines of this song repay me in an elation, almost of exquisite anguish, whenever I hear them sung by Negro children" (James Weldon Johnson).[19]

Please note this was written a few years before Teddy Roosevelt gave Johnson an appointment in the US government; more than a decade before Woodrow Wilson resegregated the federal government. I believe these words speak of progress made by the freed slaves and hope for a better tomorrow.

I am not in favor of replacing the Star-Spangled Banner as the national anthem. It has lost the meaning those earlier Jim Crow Progressives intended long ago. At the same time, I believe we need to bring "Lift Every Voice and Sing" into common public use. Let the words that James Weldon Johnson wrote unite us to throw off the intellectual shackles placed by the elites of society. After all, these lyrics have words the elites hate, such as liberty, faith, God, and the phrase "true to our native land." Let's Honor

James Weldon Johnson and his brother by making "Lift Every Voice and Sing" the "Battle Hymn of the Republic" for the twenty-first century. Together let us "trample out the vintage where our grapes of wrath" originate.

<u>Lift Every Voice and Sing</u>
Lift every voice and sing
Till earth and heaven ring,
Ring with the harmonies of Liberty;
Let our rejoicing rise
High as the listening skies,
Let it resound loud as the rolling sea.
Sing a song full of the faith that the dark past has taught us,
Sing a song full of the hope that the present has brought us.
Facing the rising sun of our new day begun,
Let us march on till victory is won.

Stony the road we trod,
Bitter the chastening rod,
Felt in the days when hope unborn had died;
Yet with a steady beat,
Have not our weary feet
Come to the place for which our fathers sighed?
We have come over a way that with tears has been watered,
We have come, treading our path through the blood of the slaughtered,

Out from the gloomy past,
Till now we stand at last
Where the white gleam of our bright star is cast.

God of our weary years,
God of our silent tears,
Thou who hast brought us thus far on the way;
Thou who hast by Thy might
Led us into the light,
Keep us forever in the path, we pray.
Lest our feet stray from the places, our God, where we
met Thee,
Lest, our hearts drunk with the wine of the world, we
forget Thee;
Shadowed beneath Thy hand,
May we forever stand.
True to our God,
True to our native land.[20]

GOODBYE MR. TANEY

In recent years many historical statues have been removed from display. I would like to address some of these removals in my adopted home state. I was surprised to learn Roger Taney was a native Marylander. I should point out that Maryland was an occupied state during the Civil War. Abraham Lincoln suspended the Writ of Habeas Corpus to arrest state politicians who wished to secede. If they had seceded, Washington, DC, would have been an island in the middle of the Confederacy. Maryland Democrats erected a statue of Roger Taney on the grounds of the State Capital outside the original front door in 1872. Even after the Civil War he was one of Maryland's favorite sons. The term Jim Crow is generally associated with the former confederate states. Could this statue have been erected as an act of defiance toward the Federal occupiers? Or was it a show of solidarity with the former confederate states during the reconstruction period. Maybe both. Taney's statue was removed from the state house grounds in August of 2017. I would rather the statues of Roger Taney and his confederate cousins had remained, and a plaque added explaining the history. As is we may forget what truly happened in the past. I'm not aware of any statues jumping from their pedestal and attacking anyone. So why did they need to be removed? In the end the push to remove the statues was an emotionally charge movement which erased an inconvenient history rather than actually address the facts.

Baltimore was a secessionist city during the Civil War. Near the city center is the Federal Hill neighborhood on the south side of the Inner Harbor. The hill was a federal gun installation during the Civil War. I've seen vintage pictures with those big guns facing toward the city.

Baltimore also placed a statue in 1887 honoring Roger Taney located in the stylish Mount Vernon neighborhood. The statue was a few blocks from the original campus of Johns Hopkins University where Woodrow Wilson received his PhD. This statue and three others were removed in August of 2017 as well. One of the other statues was of

Robert E Lee and Stonewall Jackson, two of Woodrow Wilson's favorite confederate Generals.

The Lee-Jackson statue was in the Wyman Park section of Baltimore, a then up-and-coming community near the new location of the Baltimore Museum of Art and the new campus of Johns Hopkins University. To my surprise the Lee-Jackson statue had been erected after World War II. This statue was dedicated in September 1948. At the dedication, the Mayor of Baltimore made to following speech:

"We must remain steadfast in our determination to preserve freedom, not only for ourselves, but for the other liberty-loving nations. . . Today, with our nation beset by subversive groups and propaganda which seeks to destroy our national unity, we can look for inspiration to the lives of Lee and Jackson to remind us to be resolute and determined in preserving the sacred institutions." Thomas D'Alesandro, Mayor of Baltimore[21]

The mayor's family was also in attendance including his 8-year-old daughter Nancy, the now two-time former speaker of the US House of Representatives Nancy Pelosi. I don't believe in guilt by association. I also don't know if the mayor believed what he said. I submit this as food for thought.

CHAPTER 7

PROPAGANDA FOR THE NEW AGE

As a child in the '60s, our news broadcast and magazines carried many stories about the civil rights movement. We saw the pictures of lunch counter sit-ins, marches, church bombings, and the Klan induced violence. And of course, that extra-legal enforcement group, the KKK, was around to monitor and enforce compliance with the proper social order; a social order defined by law. With the passage of the civil rights legislation of the '60s, I thought those problems were corrected and that Jim Crow came to an end.

A few years back, I had an opportunity to listen to a discussion by two people who grew up in sharecropping families in different parts of the Jim Crow south of the 1950s. One was black, the other white. I found it interesting because both groups worked in the fields. It was segregated fieldwork, blacks in one field, and whites in another, but they were allowed to associate with each other. The children could play, and parents socialize. However, when the blacks visited a white family, they had to enter by the back door because that was the "Proper Social Order" established by law. And again, the KKK would periodically be around to ensure compliance. The two are on very friendly terms today.

A common political sign today includes the statement: SCIENCE IS REAL. But sometimes science can be real evil such as the eugenics of the last century. What is the effect on a society when elites can implement such a divisive movement and pit the public against one another? How long before those divisions heal?

GASLIGHTS

Here's a strange turn as we travel down the rabbit hole. Ivan Petrovich Pavlov was born in the Czar's Russia September 26, 1849, and died February 27, 1936, in Stalin's Soviet Union. Pavlov was a world-renowned experimental neurologist, psychologist, and physiologist. His studies into classical conditioning through his experiments with dogs are common studies in universities around the world. He earned the 1904 Nobel Prize in Physiology and Medicine.

After the Russian Revolution Pavlov was praised by Lenin as his work would help them understand how to control the population. Pavlov received significant funding and was allowed to continue his work until late in life. However, Pavlov openly expressed his disapproval and contempt with which he regarded Soviet Communism. As reported in 1923, Pavlov stated "that he would not sacrifice even the hind leg of a frog to the type of social experiment that the regime was conducting in Russia."¹

In 1927, he wrote to Stalin protesting what was being done to Russian intellectuals and saying he was "ashamed to be a Russian."² That's the only account I've heard of a Soviet citizen criticizing Stalin and surviving.

My reason for this review of Ivan Pavlov is because of a personal observation some time back. I was speaking with someone whose politics differ from mine. The TV was on and set on a news channel. A report came up where a photograph was shown, and the reporter stated, "I know racism when I see it, and this is it." I heard that statement and thought, *well that's fake news* and ignored it. The other person became agitated and animated, as they believed it. My first thought was *that's like Pavlov's dogs salivating.* If I believed the reporter, I would've been upset myself.

"I have a dream that my four little children will one day live in a nation where they will not be judged by the color of their skin but by the content of their character." Dr. Martin Luther King Jr.³

As mentioned previously, Birth of a Nation became a recruiting film for the KKK of the Jim Crow Progressive common era. As such it was a propaganda tool for hate. The accusation of the film and the science of eugenics was that you could identify moral degenerates by the color of their skin. Today people are judged by the color of their skin, their genitalia, sexual orientation, the color of their clothes, or the hat they wear. How did we come to this?

Recently, we've heard charges of Jim Crow thrown around very casually. These charges bring a response of emotional indignation from some and the anger from those falsely accused. With emotional indignation, decisions are made by the heart not the head.

In today's world we have movies and television with CGI, synthesized voices, and social media all at our fingertips. In a recent 2023, interview with Tim Poole, the liberal comedian, Jimmy Dore made this statement:

> "This is the world we're living in, the stuff that we were supposed to be afraid of Donald Trump doing, Joe Biden is doing, and the corporate media gets America to cheer it on because they don't know they are the most propagandized people in the entire world."[4]

I agree with Jimmy on this, the American public is propagandized. We need to wake up, people.

With the Twitter files released in late 2022 and early 2023 we see where the FBI, CIA, DHS, CDC, Congress, etc., have been coordinating with big tech and the legacy media to sensor articles relating to Covid-19, and Hunter Biden's laptop, and election anomalies, and that Russiagate began as Clinton campaign political operation rather than Russian interference to mislead and manipulate "We the People!" It was discovered that Twitter personnel discovered the Hunter Biden laptop narrative was false and initially pushed back against the government. However, Twitter ultimately caved to government pressure and censored as requested. Additionally, Facebook personnel told the Biden campaign and the Whitehouse that covid information the Whitehouse wanted censored was accurate. Repeatedly Twitter personnel told the government the information that the government wanted censored was accurate, but ultimately caved in.[5]

Reporting by Branko Marcetic in the Jacobin, a socialist periodical, cautions those looking to disregard the Twitter files outright.

"The Twitter files give us an unprecedented peek behind the curtain at the workings of Twitter's opaque censorship regime and expose in greater detail the secret and ongoing merger of social media companies and the US national security state."

He also highlighted that: a "perplexed" Roth commented the questions were "more like something we'd get from a congressional committee than the Bureau," and declared he was not "comfortable" with the implications of "state-controlled media" they carried."[6]

Yoel Roth was the head of content moderation when Elon Musk purchased Twitter.

It was not my intent to develop a comprehensive list of free speech violations by the cabal of government and big tech and or the corporate media, only to point out that it exists. I would however question how long that has been the case.

Polls have indicated that the 2020 election results

would have been different if the Hunter Biden laptop story had not been suppressed. Upwards of 20 percent of Biden voters would have changed their vote if the New York Post story had not been suppressed.[7, 8, 9]

CHAPTER 8

SOCIALISM IN OUR MIDST

During college in the 1970s I knew there were little news-paper boxes around campus where you could get a copy of the Students for a Democratic Society, SDS, newspaper. They were free and everybody knew that they were a communist front group. I didn't take them seriously because they had a small presence. Reflecting, I expect they probably were getting support from the Soviet Union. At the time I was not aware of Whittaker Chambers who published the book "The Witness." Whittaker Chambers was an ex-communist agent recruited by the Soviet Union who had been active in Washington, DC, during the 20s and 30s. He eventually left the movement after realizing how evil communism was. Whittaker Chambers testified before Congress during the House Un-American Activities Committee hearings in the 1940s.[1]

Having lived in the Baltimore-Washington metropolitan area for over 40 years I've met numerous retired military officers. Many have shared anecdotal stories, some humorous, about life in the military. One mentioned that while serving they had an opportunity to attend a lecture by a former KGB general. The KGB general asserted that Senator Joseph McCarthy was right and also wrong. He claimed that Senator McCarthy was right that the Soviet Union had agents within the US government. He was wrong in that he identified some folks who were not involved.

In the April 14, 1996, Washington Post article titled "Was McCarthy Right About the Left?" Micholas von Hoffman reported on several sources confirming this fact. First, the early 1990's records from Moscow's Russian Center for the Preservation and Study of Documents of Recent history provided proof that the Soviet Government subsidized the Communist Party USA which served as a base for serious espionage. Beginning in the 1940s a top-secret NSA program, Venona, intercepted communications between Moscow and its American agents. When translated years later Venona transcripts showed that the Roosevelt (FDR) and Truman administrations were riddled with communist spies and political operatives.[2]

During a 1984 interview KGB defector Yuri Bezmenov described KGB manipulation of US public opinion. He explained that the KGB used ideological subversion on the US population. He stated that:

> "Ideologic Subversion is the legitimate, overt and open process, you can see it with your own eyes, all American media has to do is to unplug the bananas from their ears, open up their eyes and they can see it. In reality the main emphasis of the KGB is not in intelligence at all....only

about 15 percent of time money and manpower is spent on espionage as such. The other 85 percent is a slow process which we call either Ideological Subversion or active measures or psychological warfare. What it basically means is to change the perception of reality of every American to such an extent that in spite of an abondance of information no one is able to come to sensible conclusions in the interest in defending themselves, their family, their community, and their country. It's a great brainwashing process which goes very slow and is divided into four basic stages.

The first stage being demoralization. It takes about fifteen to twenty years to demoralize a nation. Why that number of years? Because this is the minimum number of years it requires to educate one generation of students.... exposed to the ideology of your enemy.

The second stage is destabilization....it takes only from 2 to 5 years to destabilize a nation... in such sensitive areas as defense and economy the influence of Marxist/ Leninist ideas in the United States is absolutely fantastic.

The third stage is of course crisis. It may take only up to six weeks to bring a country to the verge of crisis. You can see it Central America now (1984).

The fourth stage is normalization. After crisis, with a violent change of power structure and economy, you have the so-called period of normalization. It may last indefinitely... to eliminate the principle of free market competition and to put a big brother government in Washington, DC."³

In 1984, Bezmenov was saying the first stage was already complete stating:

"The result, the result you can see most of the people who graduated in '60s dropouts or half-baked intellectuals are now occupying the positions of power in the government, civil service, business, mass media, educational system. You are stuck with them; you cannot get rid of them. They are contaminated, they are programmed to think and react to certain stimuli in a certain pattern. You cannot change their mind even if you expose them to authentic information."[4]

Bezmenov was correct regarding stage one. Many of the '60s radicals remained on campus and became faculty and administrators. But it takes time for those earlier generations to move from power to the institutions Bezmenov mentioned

President Ronald Reagan famously stated his strategy toward the Soviet Union. "Here's my strategy on the Cold War: We win, they lose."[5]

President Reagan embarked on a military buildup that ultimately the Soviets couldn't keep up with. This is one of the many causes of the fall of the Soviet Union. After the Soviet bloc broke up and the Berlin Wall fell, conservatives celebrated the fall of communism. Until this point, we really hadn't spoken much about a threat from China or the remnants of Soviet influence remaining in the US. Those Soviet agents and/or sympathizers who had worked their way into the US government, American universities, media outlets, and cultural institutions remained entrenched and parasitically feeding on the American host. Today's universities are promoting socialism, also known as communism, as a good form of government.[6,7]

This effort, on the part of the Soviet Union, was picked up by China in recent years. By buying influence in American institutions, academia, news, entertainment, and government, China has become very successful given the divisions in our politics and society in general.[8]
Sadly, whether communist or fascist, socialism has almost always gone badly. We can see that with Venezuela as the latest example but most countries in Latin America have been destabilized by past socialist governments.

Let's review a few of the past socialist horrors.

- Venezuela: Hugo Chavez was democratically elected in 1999 promising power to the people. Chavez quickly brought about reforms, abolishing checks and balances of authority enshrined in the previously constitution. He evolved into a dictator and the day he died he was the wealthiest man in Venezuela. The day after he died his daughter, Maria, was a wealthiest person in Venezuela, and still is with $4.2 billion.[9] Meanwhile the people are having to escape the country for lack of food. They don't have pets any longer because they've eaten them! Even Hitler was duly elected, but only once.[10]
- Cambodia: Pol Pott took over Cambodia and millions

of people were exterminated in Cambodia's killing fields. Sometimes you just have to get a little heavy-handed with people who don't quite see your plan for government.[11]

- Cuba: Fidel Castro took over Cuba in 1958. Professor Armando Lago estimated the number of Cubans killed during his revolution to be in the tens of thousands but is more likely to be closer to one hundred thousand. Armando Lago was a Harvard-trained economist who spent years studying what the revolution cost the people of Cuba.[12]

- China: Chairman Mao came to power in 1948. A former Communist Party official (while working at Princeton University) said that 80 million died unnatural deaths, most the result of famine following the Great Leap Forward.[13] Of all socialist dictators, Mao was the deadliest of all the world dictators. Implementing communist policies Mao starved possibly as many as 80 million people. Mao had many intellectuals who disagreed with him, he put people in labor camps. He condoned beating and stoning people to death in struggle sessions.[14]

- Germany: The National Socialist German Workers Part, Nazis, and Adolf Hitler came to power in 1932. Their intent was to establish his master race to rule the world. It's estimated the Nazis/Hitler killed 30 million people. The best-known aspect of this is the Holocaust, which killed six million Jews. Hitler also ordered the less well-known General plan Ost, which resulted in a genocide of millions of Slavic people by starvation. Nazis considered the Slaves to be an inferior race. This resulted in the deaths of between 4.5 and 13.7 million people. In total the holocaust killed potentially 17 million people if you include non-Jews.[15]

- Soviet Union: When Lenin, the founder of the Soviet Union, USSR, died, Joseph Stalin took power. Joseph Stalin was in power from 1929 to 1953. Stalin is the most infamous communist dictator. In the first twelve years Stalin lead the Soviet Union, horrible atrocities were committed in Gulags and the collective farms resulting in the deaths of between forty and sixt-two million people. Stalin's Gulags were a series of forced labor camps where he sent political dissidents to work as slaves. Many worked until they died of exhaustion.[16]

The collective farm was Stalin's concept to modernize Soviet agriculture by consolidating traditional small farms into large collectives. The intent was to adopt modern agricultural techniques, hence increase production. However, many peasants resented collectivization. The government's response was a campaign of propaganda, coercion, and violence. The peasants who resisted were labelled "Kulaks" and could be arrested and imprisoned or executed. A series of devastating famines resulted in millions of deaths in the USSR.[17] During the Holodomor, Stalin stole food from Ukraine, and then blocked off the country, forcing them to starve in order to subjugate any national-istic ideas.[18] There is one more philosophy to discuss, but first let's review the two primary forms of socialism.

MARXIST SOCIALISM: COMMUNISM

Karl Marx, a German philosopher, wrote his Communist Manifesto in 1848. In its pages he outlined his ideas for a utopian society. Marx believed the emphasis on private ownership and profit that was intrinsic to capitalism lead to inequalities in society. His goal was to promote a con-cept for a classless society where everyone shared in the benefits of labor with the state controlling all property and wealth; a society in which no one was motivated by greed or tried to rise above others. The belief was that Communism would end worker exploitation, close the wealth gap, and free the poor from oppression.[19]

The atrocities committed during the rise of the Soviet Union, USSR, were many. Millions of people were betrayed and died as a result. Marx is famous for his statement reli-gion an "Opiate of the People."

In his "Critique of Hegel's Philosophy of Right" Marx states:

"Religious distress is at the same time the expression of real distress and the protest against real distress. Religion is the sigh of the oppressed creature, the heart of a heart-less world, just as it is the spirit of a spiritless situation. It is the opium of the people. The abolition of religion as the illusory happiness of the people is required for their real happiness. The demand to give up the illusion about its condition is the demand to give up a condition which needs illusions."[20]

When Lenin and Stalin implemented communism in the USSR, they murdered priests and religious adherents and demolished churches. The Communists took over businesses and agriculture, placing true believers in communism in charge, most of whom did not have a clue about business operation. And shortages began.

A NEW AND IMPROVED SOCIALISM: FASCISM

A committed Marxist Socialist, Benito Mussolini observed flaws in the implementation of communism in the USSR and developed his new concept for the socialist utopia.

"Fascism should more properly be called corporatism because it is the merger of state and corporate power." Benito Mussolini[21]

The Fascist philosophy considers private enterprise to be the most effective tool in the sphere of production and hence a useful instrument in the interest of the nation. The private enterprise is therefore responsible to the state and its direction given to production. The state only interferes when economic production is insufficient or when the political interests of the State dictate.[22]

Communist and Fascist parties rose in countries around Europe between 1922 and 1945. The most prominent was the Nazis of Adolf Hitler's National Socialist German Workers Party. Mussolini's Fascist Italy did not embrace antisemitism until 1938 in order to solidify his military alliance with Hitler. Fascists were known to be opportunistic, and willing to change in official party positions in order to win elections.

Most European countries still have an official state church.[23] In Hitler's Germany the Lutheran Church was the state church. Lutherans were required to display pictures of Hitler and replace the cross with Swastikas. Pastors were monitored to ensure they did not criticize the government.

NO HONOR AMONG SOCIALISTS

The public-school education I received discussed our alliance with the Soviet Union during World War Two. Recently, I was surprised to learn of the pact between the Nazis and the Soviets dividing up Poland. This nonaggression pact would allow the Nazis to take over the western portions of Europe and the Soviets to fight the Japanese in the west and take over the Eastern Europe without having to worry about war on another front.

Officially called the Molotov-Ribbentrop Pact, also known as the Hitler-Stalin Pact, the nonaggression agreement was simple and straightforward. Both countries pledged for 10 years to desist from any act of violence, any aggressive action, and any attack on each other, either individually or jointly with other powers.[24]

President Franklin D. Roosevelt warned Stalin stating, "It was as certain as that the night followed the day that as soon as Hitler had conquered France he would turn on Russia and it would be the Soviets' turn next."

How true. On June 22, 1941, Hitler launched the largest surprise attack in the history of warfare, Operation Barbarossa.[25, 26]

You could say there is no honor among socialists. This was before the American public fully understood the atrocities the Nazis were perpetrating.

As a free and open society, the United States was exposed to Soviet influence. Penetration of government, academia, the media, and Hollywood was a priority for Stalin. Over many decades that penetration was successful. As previously discussed, the Soviet Union was infiltrating our institutions while at the same time we were allied against the axis powers.

In 1975 during an interview with Mike Wallace, Ronald Reagan stated:

"Someone very profoundly once said, many years ago, that if Fascism ever comes to America it will come in the name of liberalism. What is fascism? Fascism is private ownership, private enterprise, but total government control and regulation. Well, isn't this the liberal philosophy. The conservative so-called is the one, is the one that says less government, get off my back, get out of my pocket, and let me have more control of my own destiny."[27]

This philosophy is demonstrated in the American political environment today. The Democratic party, the party of the expert elitist, constantly expands government in order to get greater control of the lives of the average American. This began with Teddy Roosevelt, Republican, and greatly intensified under Woodrow Wilson, Democrat, during the Jim Crow Progressive Common Era. The Republican Party today is promoting individual freedom and getting the government out of our lives. To rephrase, one party believes that certain people are superior and should plan other people's lives, the other party believes that people should be free to plan their own lives.

In the Soviet Union, the government took control of the means of production. It then eliminated the "bourgeoisie" that had run industry or farms/agriculture. As a result, production plummeted. As the people found it harder to feed themselves, the government cracked down on the unrest of the people and didn't change direction. The fascists took note and left businesses in private hands but demanded that they meet government regulations/directions/objectives. Either way there is an elitist class in the government planning the society.

THIRD FORM OF SOCIALISM

For my entire life I thought I lived in a Democratic Republic where the people voted for their government and enjoyed a high degree of freedom. Researching this book has changed my thinking. I believe we have been operating under a peculiarly American form of socialism for over a century. A socialism which began as "corporatism" with Republican and Democratic Progressives in the early 1900s, about a decade before Benito Mussolini defined fascism in Italy. A socialism with degrees of freedom varied with time and population subgroups, but always enough freedom to keep a large portion of an unsuspecting public from realizing how we've been manipulated. A socialism with constant tension between progressive/liberal politicians expanding government and conservatives who try to restrain the power of the state. Like communism and fascism, this American form of socialism resulted in an administrative state that acts to ensure its self-preservation; an administrative state that will strike out against perceived threats to power.

For decades the progressives/liberals have been falsely labeling all conservatives as racists, white supremacists, Nazis, and their ilk. I knew this was wrong simply because I don't feel this way. Long ago I realized progressives/liberals were profiling conservatives this way because they couldn't defend the results of their own policies. This fact is clear if you look at the conditions of the poor in American cities. Furthermore, liberals tend to put those same labels on black Republicans as well, sometimes calling them race traitors simply because they don't agree on policies or concepts. This extreme profiling is not new. The 1915 movie *Birth of a Nation* drove home the idea that black men were going to rape white women.

Let's not forget that famous quote by Southern Democrat Lyndon Baines Johnson in 1963.

"These Negroes, they're getting pretty uppity these days and that's a problem for us since they've got something now, they never had before, the political pull to back up their uppityness. Now we've got to do something about this, we've got to give them a little something, just enough to quiet them down, not enough to make a difference...I'll have them n...s voting Democratic for the next two hundred years."[28]

The Great Society followed.

Johnson also said:

"The family is the corner stone of our society. More than any other force it shapes the attitude, the hopes, the ambitions, and the values of the child. And when the family collapses it is the children that are usually damaged. When it happens on a massive scale the community itself is crippled." Lyndon B. Johnson[29]

I don't know when Lyndon Johnson said this, but he did not live long enough to see the damage the Great Society programs would do. In 1965 Daniel Patrick Moynihan first raised a concern in his report: "The Negro Family: The Case for National Action." Following are a couple of excerpts from this report:

"The role of the family in shaping character and ability is so pervasive as to be easily overlooked. The family is the basic social unit of American life; it is the basic socializing unit. By and large, adult conduct in society is learned as a child."

"There is considerable evidence that the Negro community is in fact dividing between a stable middle-class group that is steadily growing stronger and more successful, and an increasingly disorganized and disadvantaged lower-class group."[30]

In 2013, nearly fifty years later NPR revisited the report and made the following comments.

Moynihan often reeled off the dire statistics(1960's):

"About a quarter of Negro families are headed by women. The divorce rate is about 2 1/2 times what it is [compared with whites]," Moynihan said. "The number of fatherless children keeps growing. And all these things keep getting worse, not better, over recent years." [31]

Since the release of the Moynihan report, significant progress has been made for middle-class blacks, but there has been little economic improvement for the black poor; the same disparities Moynihan noticed 50 years ago remain in place today.

Years later, the problem remains large enough for a concerned father–President Obama–to address the nation: "We got single moms out here. They're heroic what they're doing. We're so proud of them," Obama said, "but at the same time, I wish I'd had a father who was around and involved."[32]

Moynihan joined the Kennedy administration as Assistant Secretary of Labor for Policy, Planning and Research in 1963.[33] The Moynihan Report was published in March of 1965. As such his comments and analysis were based on the results of previous policies and actions, as Lyndon Johnson began promoting his "Great Society" programs in March of 1964 but were not yet in effect.

Thomas Sowell has stated the following:

"As of 1960, two-thirds of all black American children were living with both parents. That declined over the years, until only one-third were living with both parents in 1995.... Among black families in poverty 85 percent of the children had no father present."[34]

Sowell goes on to explain an impact of the Welfare State:

"...It makes it unnecessary for fathers to support their offspring. In fact it makes it counterproductive in many cases. A very poor man who might be able to support his family may realize his family will be better off without him. But on the other hand, someone who's strictly irresponsible either the man or the woman or both, now pays no price for being irresponsible the taxpayers pay the price. And actually, the harm done to the taxpayers, which is serious, still is not comparable to the harm done to the people, to the families and especially the children. Moynihan was excoriated for pointing this out."[35]

Sowell also points out that Moynihan was speaking from experience as:

"Moynihan was a scholar who knew that his own group, the Irish Americans, had that very same problem at the beginning of the twentieth century. And more importantly Moynihan's own father deserted the family when he was 10 years old."[36]

I think the result we're struggling from today should have been predictable. Remember, there are problems that go back generations. The black community as a collective was improving their status from the Civil War until the Jim Crow Progressive Common Era. During my research I did not find any discussion connecting the issues of concern to policies from the Jim Crow Progressive Common Era. But then the "confession" from The Harvard Review discussed earlier is a recent development. Remember, Irish Catholics were targets of bigotry and discrimination during the Jim Crow Progressive Common Era as well.

As American whites turned from their previous "gas-lit" bigotry (i.e., *Birth of a Nation*, eugenics...) the ruling elite needed some other means to maintain control/power. I believe the story of the big switch, where racist southern Democrats became Republicans, was told and used as a tool to divide and distract.

Over four decades ago, Thomas Sowell discussed poverty and dependence with William F. Buckley on the Show "Firing Line" on PBS November 12, 1981. Following are some excerpts of Mr. Sowell's comments I believe are pertinent.

"Unfortunately, politics involves telling people what they want to hear, and what people want to hear is that a certain kind of villainy can explain almost all of it. Now there's no such thing as a lack of villainy among human beings. Anytime you take any large group of people you have an almost inexhaustible source of sins. And if you want to look into all those sins, you can go on forever looking into them. The question is whether those sins explain the numbers you're talking about."[37]

Sowell's comments regarded how group history impacted group performance.

"...the Jews who came here came with all sorts of urban skills. They were clothing industries, garment work that sort of thing. The Germans came here with all sorts of skill and beer-making, piano making, machinery kinds of things. Blacks of course emerging from slavery had enormous disadvantages. Even as compared to people emerging from slavery in other parts of the Western Hemisphere. Because, for one thing in the United States the blacks were not allowed to have any responsibilities under slavery. That was one of the keyways of holding blacks in slavery at low cost was to keep the people dependent as much as possible. Now people try to do that in other parts of the Western Hemisphere. It wasn't as possible, say in the West Indies, because there weren't enough whites for example in the West Indies to matter. So, if blacks were going to be fed the West Indies, they had to be fed by growing their own food...blacks in the West Indies had all sorts of experience growing their own food selling the surplus in the market and in fact being responsible for budgeting what they had. Blacks in the United States were deliberately kept from having that. Dependence was seen as the key to holding the slaves down. It's ironic that same principle comes up in the welfare state a hundred years later."[38]

Sowell's comments continued regarding politicians and policy effectiveness.

".... Politics really involves getting people to vote for you. And people vote for you when they think that they can depend on you when they are dependent on you. To the extent that people become self-reliant and can feel they're perfectly capable of taking care of themselves, to that extent do you lose your hold on their votes... there are people who are professional politicians who simply look at the bottom line, where the votes go. There are other people who sincerely believe that if they will hand out things here and there that this will in fact benefit people...I haven't been able to find a single country in the world where the policies that are being advocated for blacks the United States have lifted any people out of poverty. I've seen many examples around the world people who began in poverty and ended in affluence. Not one of them has followed any pattern at all like what is being advocated for blacks in the United States. Many groups have remained in poverty for a very long time trying to follow those patterns."[39]

Sowell stated that several ways government policies make getting a foot hold in the job market difficult.

"...Minimum wage law would be one of those things but only one. The terrible schooling would be a major factor, that if you're trying to turn out kids 40 percent functionally illiterate upon graduation from high school then you're going to have very serious problems in the job market...The government runs the schools, state as well as federal. They're doing many things to make it much tougher for the person at the bottom to get started. And they're (the government) also making it less necessary to get started by having various subsidy programs, food stamps, welfare and so on, which reduce the difference between working and not working. So that the general tendency of what they're doing is to make it harder to rise, but of course if you're lucky enough to have started to rise before these programs began then you're in great shape."[40]

In the over four decades since this program, the effects of globalization and outsourcing of American industry, once thriving factories in America's cities have been shuttered. At the same time the elites of both political parties have become wealthy. I will speak more to in the final chapter.

THE FRANKFURT SCHOOL

The Frankfurt School was a group of researchers associated with the Institute for Social Research in Frankfurt am Main, Germany, who applied Marxism to a radical interdisciplinary social theory. Founded by Carl Grünberg in 1923, "The Institute for Social Research" began at The University of Frankfurt. This was the first Marxist-oriented research center affiliated with a major German university.

Frankfurt School members tried to develop a social theory based on Marxism and Hegelian philosophy while also utilizing the aspects of psychoanalysis, sociology, existential philosophy, and other disciplines. Utilizing Marxist concepts, they would analyze the social relationships in capitalist economic systems. The result known as "critical theory," yielded influential critiques of the greater society. Fascism and authoritarianism were prominent subjects of study as well.

With the rise to power of Adolf Hitler and the Nazis most of the institute's scholars were forced to leave Germany. Many moved to the United States and The Institute for Social Research found a home at Columbia University until 1949, when it returned to Frankfurt. Many of the "critical theorists" remained in the United States. During the 1950s the critical theorists of the Frankfurt School diverged in several intellectual directions. Most of them disavowed orthodox Marxism, however remained highly critical of capitalism.[41]

CHAPTER 9
CHRISTIAN NATIONALISM, OH MY!

In the movie "The Wizard of Oz" on her journey to The Emerald City Dorothy meets a Tin Man and a Scare Crow. They agree to travel the Yellow Brick Road together. They hope the Tin Man can get a brain, the Scarecrow a heart and Dorothy can get home to Kansas and Auntie Em.

As they travel through a dark wood they begin to worry about threats in the woods. As they walk forward, they chant "Lions and Tigers and Bears! Oh My! Lions and Tigers and Bears! Oh My! Lions and Tigers and Bears! Oh My!" faster and faster as the fear builds. Suddenly, a ferocious lion jumps out of the woods snarling and snapping piquing their fears. After a brief exchange they discovered the lion was a coward, even afraid of his own shadow. They become friends and proceed to the Emerald City with the added goal of getting the lion some courage.[1] In the land of Oz the threat came from their minds not the cowardly lion.

The Jim Crow Progressives of the late 19th and early twentieth century developed a divisive narrative. A narrative that stated certain people were less intelligent, were predisposed to criminal behavior, and were innately dishonest, and you could identify those people because their skin was black. These early progressives also promoted the idea that Catholics could not be trusted in American life as they followed the Pope, a foreign religious leader. They were creating a narrative which they could use to say, "Ah-ha, see them? They're bad, evil, criminal..." The result? They sowed distrust and suspicion into society.

In recent years progressives tried the narrative that all white people are racists, an attempt to distract from the reality that the problems in our inner cities are primarily the result of policies of college educated politicians, and not just white politicians. I was recently challenged about my Christian beliefs and was exposed to a whole new narrative which I believe was developed by progressives to scare their supporters. The protagonist was quite agitated. So here we go again.

So, what is the new boogeyman narrative? Christian Nationalism! This term was new to me, and I was blindsided. It was time to research. There are many long-standing problems throughout the country which long-time politicians have not resolved. I assume a "nationalist" would prioritize internal problems over the world's problems.

Numerous articles report on a narrative written by The Public Religion Research Institute and the liberal Brookings Institute. One article even referred to Christian

Nationalism as Christo-fascist worldview.[2] The report is based on a survey carefully crafted and interpreted to present their political opponents in the worst light. They wouldn't have published if it had it not. Following are some headlines from articles written by likeminded individuals:

- Troubling data shows many Americans are pining to become a theocracy[3]
- The Growing Anti-Democratic Threat of Christian Nationalism in the US[4]
- Christian nationalism is still thriving—and is a force for returning Trump to power[5]
- Christian Nationalism Is "Single Biggest Threat" to America's Religious Freedom[6]

PRRI asked respondents to agree or disagree with five statements to draw out this dangerous new movement and frighten the likeminded. Here they are:

1. The US government should declare America a Christian nation.
2. U.S. laws should be based on Christian values.
3. If the US moves away from our Christian foundations, we will not be a country anymore.
4. Being Christian is an important part of being American.
5. God has called Christians to exercise dominion over all areas of American society.[7]

I don't plan to address these questions which were carefully crafted to support a biased result. Instead, I'm going to look at examples of actual Christian Nationalism.

THE FOUNDING FATHERS

The American Revolution occurred during a spiritual revival in the British colonies in North America.[8, 9] Out of this revival came the premise that our rights come from God not the King as enshrined in "The Declaration of Independence." Many, but not all, of the founding fathers were Christians. The American Revolution was fought not only for religious freedom but freedom in general. They were attempting something new—a nation of, by and for the people. The signers of the Declaration knew that the crown would consider this declaration an act of treason, therefore, they pledged "Their Lives, Fortunes and Sacred Honor" to the cause. Some did pay with their life.

JOHN BROWN

John Brown led a movement of extremist Christian abolitionist insurrectionists. Brown led raids against pro-slavery forces throughout the nation including "Bloody Kansas". Brown and his band were captured during a raid of the federal arsenal in Harper's Ferry, West Virginia, and hanged by Robert E. Lee.[10]

UNION TROOPS

Abolitionists were inspired by the "Christ-like" image of Uncle Tom, the suffering servant that died for two runaways and founded the Republican party as an anti-slavery party. The Union Army march theme song was the "Battle Hymn of The Republic," a spectacular theme for Christian warriors "stamping out the vintage where the grapes of wrath were stored."

JIM CROW PROGRESSIVE MOVEMENT

This movement saw the United States as a nation for white protestants, many extremely devoted to their Christian faith. They were also devoted to the science of white supremacy, eugenics. During this period the KKK was resurrected in support of Woodrow Wilson's segregationist policies. They followed their science to an extreme. With the new media of silent film, "The Birth of a Nation" spread fear across the land. As stated previously Benito Mussolini defined fascism thusly. "Fascism should more properly be called corporatism because it is the merger of state and corporate power," which is to say government experts set policies that the corporations are required to follow. That is the relationship between government and business in our economy today. Fortunately, after a few years the American public rejected this brand of Christian Nationalism!

WWI AND WWII VETERANS

The Christian Negro troops of WWI and WWII who self-lessly stepped forward to fight to prove their ability, despite the Jim Crow Progressivism of the day, many now populate American cemeteries in Europe. The Christian white troops of WWI and WWII also selflessly stepped forward to stop aggression of the national socialists and many now populate American cemeteries in Europe.

Following are several examples I consider Christian Nationalism in Hitler's Germany.

DIETRICH BONHOEFFER

Dietrich Bonhoeffer was a member of the German Evangelical Lutheran Church. Before Hitler's rise to power, Bonhoeffer had made international contacts in the Protestant ecumenical movement. As a result of the chaos of the Weimar years many Protestant leaders welcomed the rise of Nazism. Likewise, many German Christians wanted Protestantism to conform to the ideology of the godless National Socialists. Bonhoeffer argued that they were surrendering Christian precepts to political ideology.

The more traditional protestants formed the Confessing Church in May 1934 to separate from the predominant German Christians. Most members of the Confessing Church remained silent regarding the National Socialist persecution of the Jews as a means of self-preservation. They did not wish to draw attention to themselves in this nasty socialist state. Bonhoeffer used his social connections to help clergy of the Confessing Church to avoid military service. He also established an illegal secret seminary to train young clergy.

To avoid military service himself, Bonhoeffer became involved in military intelligence, the Abwehr, a group interested in rescuing Jews and overthrowing the Nazi regime. Dietrich Bonhoeffer and his co-conspirators were eventually captured by the Gestapo. Dietrich Bonhoeffer was executed April 9, 1945, as were others. Christian Nationalists–German Style.[11]

SOPHIE SCHOLL AND THE WHITE ROSE

The despair and instability of the Weimar Republic made difficult years for the German people. When the Nazis gained power in 1933, Sophie and many of her siblings became avid members of the National Socialist youth cult. Sophie and many of her contemporaries were enamored with the focus on nature and communal experiences. Sophie joined the League of German Girls and quickly rose in the ranks. A devote man firmly grounded in Christian tradition Sophie's father, Robert Scholl viewed the developments in German society with fear and horror. The dinner table was a place of lively discussion where Robert would teach his children the value of open and honest conversation.

Because of their faith, Sophie's brother Hans and some of his friends came to question the Nazi system and began distributing flyers in resistance which they distributed around Munich. Sophie eventually got involved as well.

"Our current 'state' is the dictatorship of evil. We know that already, I hear you object, and we don't need you to reproach us for it yet again. But, I ask you, if you know that, then why don't you act? Why do you tolerate these rulers gradually robbing you, in public and in private, of one right after another, until one day nothing, absolutely nothing, remains but the machinery of the state, under the command of criminals and drunkards?" Third White Rose Pamphlet.[12]

In later White Rose Pamphlets they advocated for sabotage of Hitler's war machine.

"And now every convinced opponent of National Socialism must ask himself how he can fight against the present 'state' in the most effective way... We cannot provide each man with the blueprint for his acts, we can only suggest them in general terms, and he alone will find the way of achieving this end: Sabotage in armament plants and war industries, sabotage at all gatherings, rallies, public ceremonies, and organizations of the National Socialist Party. Obstruction of the smooth functioning of the war machine... Try to convince all your acquaintances...of the senselessness of continuing, of the hopelessness of this war; of our spiritual and economic enslavement at the hands of the National Socialists; of the destruction of all moral and religious values; and urge them to passive resistance!" Fifth With Rose Pamphlet[13]

Eventually while distributing White Rose pamphlets Sophie, Hans, and their Compatriots were caught and turned over to the Gestapo. After a half-day mock trial Sophie, Hans, and others were sentenced to death for treason. When asked if she regretted her conduct Sophie replied,

"I am, now as before, of the opinion that I did the best that I could do for my nation. I therefore do not regret my conduct and will bear the consequences that result from my conduct."[14]

Sophie, Hans, and Christoph Probst were executed by guillotine on February 22, 1943.[15, 16] Christian Nationalism—German Style.

These examples of the German Christian Nationalism represent people who made the ultimate sacrifice standing up to the National Socialist German Workers Party, the Nazis. Thus, German Christians who embraced Nazism may also have been very nationalistic. However, to embrace Nazism they were rejecting their "Jewish Savior" and embracing Adolph Hitler. Were they still Christians? I think not. In Hitler's Germany the National Socialists were the Nasties!

It was ten to fifteen years ago that I learned the progressive mantra had risen over America's universities once again. If someone wants the mantra, shouldn't they accept the history as their own? I don't believe the progressives ever went away; they just took a low profile for a while. Are progressives in fact continuing to pursue the science of eugenics? Some think they are. Is the genetic technology used to create covid-19 in fact eugenics?[17, 18]

CHAPTER 10
IMMIGRATION REFORM

1986 SIMPSON MAZZOLI IMMIGRATION BILL

When Ronald Reagan entered office in 1981, he was concerned with the immigration problems left over from the Carter administration, specifically, the Cubans from the Mariel boatlift and a large group of Haitians.[1] I remember that Castro had emptied his prisons and shipped his prisoners to the US. President Reagan considered the Cuban and Haitian issue the more significant driver for immigration reform. The Reagan administration proposed full legal status for illegal immigrants under the term "renewable term temporary resident."[2]

In 1981, the Reagan team began working with Congress on a bill that included penalties for employers hiring unknown undocumented immigrants. This bill titled the Simpson Mazzoli Immigration bill for its authors Republican Alan Simpson and Democrat Romano Mazzoli was signed by President Reagan.[3]

The bill made any immigrant who'd entered the

country before 1982 eligible for amnesty; nearly three million illegal immigrants which was approximately twice the number the government estimated prior to passage of the bill. Yet the law was largely considered unsuccessful because the strict sanctions on employers were stripped out of the bill for passage.[4] Without the employer sanctions, amnesty became an illegal immigration magnet.

During the 1984 presidential debate President Regan said:

"... it is true our borders are out of control. It is also true that this has been a situation in our borders back through a number of administrations. And I supported this bill. I believe in the idea of amnesty for those who have put down roots and have lived here even though some time back they may have entered illegally. With regard to the employer sanctions, we must have that. Not only to ensure that we can identify the illegal aliens but also while some keep protesting about what it would do to employers, there is another employer that we shouldn't be so concerned about. And these are employers down through the years who have encouraged the illegal entry into this country because they then hire these individuals and hire them at starvation wages and none of the benefits, that we think our normal and natural for workers in our country and the individuals can't complain because of their illegal status. We don't think that those people should be allowed to continue operating free, and this was why the provisions we had in with regard to sanctions and so forth. And I'm going to do everything I can and all of us in the administration are join in again when Congress is back at it to get an immigration bill that will give us once again control of our borders."[5, 6]

During the same debate Walter Mondale stated:

"...I object to that part of the Simpson Mazzoli bill which I think is very unfair and would prove to be so. That is the part that requires employers to determine the citizenship of an employee before they're hired. I am convinced that the result of this would be the people who are Hispanic, people have different languages, or speak with an accent difficult to be employed. I think that's wrong we've never had citizenship test in our country before and I don't think we should have a citizenship card today. That is counterproductive.

I do support the other aspects of the Simpson Mazzoli bill that strengthen enforcement at the border, strengthen other ways of dealing with undocumented workers in this difficult area. And dealing with the problem of settling who have lived here for many, many years and do not have an established status. I further strongly recommend that this administration do something it has not done. That is to strengthen enforcement at the border, strengthen the officials in this government that deal with undocumented workers and to do so in a way that is responsible and within the constitution of the United States. We need an answer to this problem, but it must be an American answer that is consistent with justice and due process..."[7]

Panelist Georgie Anne Geyer of UPS pointed asked the following:

"Sir, people as well-balanced and just as Father Theodor Hesburgh of Notre Dame who headed the select commission on immigration, have pointed out repeatedly that there will be no immigration reform without employer sanctions. Because it would be an unbalanced bill and there would be simply no way to reinforce it...Your critics have also said repeatedly that you have not gone along with the bill or any immigration reform because of the Hispanic groups, or Hispanic leadership groups, who actually do not represent what the Hispanic Americans want because polls show that they overwhelmingly want some kind of immigration reform. How can you justify your position on this? And how do you respond to the criticism that this is an example of your flip-flopping and giving in to special interest groups at the expense of the American nations?"[8]

Mondale responded: "...this bill imposes on employers the responsibility of determining whether somebody who applies for a job is an American or not. And just inevitably they're going be reluctant to hire Hispanics or people with a different accent..."

Mondale went on to restate his concern for the employers

being made responsible for determining citizenship status. Mondale also stated the polls show the American people want the employer verification he rejects. But unlike Reagan, he expressed no concern for the immigrants potentially being abused and mistreated.

In 2010 Reagan's former speech writer Peter Robinson stated:

> "He, too, would have been right there in saying, 'Fix the borders first.' That the US failed to regain control of the border—making the 1986 law's amnesty provision an incentive for others to come to America illegally—would have infuriated Reagan."[9]

JORDAN COMMISSION RECOMMENDATIONS

The Immigration Act of 1990 stipulated that a bipartisan commission be created with the objectives to 1) examine the impacts of immigration on the United States, and 2) make recommendations on immigration policy. President Bill Clinton had appointed chair Barbara Jordan. Jordan held a press conference in 1995 to release the Commission's recommendations on legal immigration.[10]

The Jordan Commission Recommendations to Prevent Illegal Immigration, compiled by FAIR, include:[11]

· Border management needs to be reinforced to prevent illegal immigration and facilitate legal entries. Increased resources are necessary for additional

Border Patrol officers, inspectors, and operational support.

- Employment magnets for illegal aliens need to be eliminated through worksite enforcement. Economic gains and employment prospects are major pull factors of immigrants- including over-stayers. As Jordan (1995) noted, "roughly one-half of the nation's illegal alien problem results from visitors who entered legally but who do not leave when their time is up. Let me tell you in three simple words why that is: they get jobs..."

- Eligibility of illegal aliens for publicly funded services or assistance (except those made available on an emergency basis) is ruled out: "Decisions about eligibility should support our immigration objectives. Accordingly, the Commission recommended against eligibility for illegal aliens 'except in most unusual circumstances...'" (Jordan 1995).

- Coordinated strategies with foreign governments to address the causes of illegal immigration in sending countries. This can be done through development programs to reduce the push factors of migration. Coordination with Mexico is fundamental, given its geographical proximity to the United States and its large flow of migrants.

- Increase the capacity in detention centers to facilitate the processing and removal of deportable aliens. A credible immigration policy requires the deportation of immigrants who have no right of residence.

Going from the premise that "unlawful immigration is unacceptable," the Commission warned against rewarding illegal aliens. If aliens believe they can remain in the States indefinitely, they will be encouraged to enter or reside illegally.
· Amnesty is out of the question and "deportation is crucial."

The Jordan Commission Recommendations on Immigrant Admissions, compiled by FAIR, include:[12]

· Reduce immigrant admission by thirty percent (from 822,000 to 550,000 admissions per year).
· Favor the admission of skilled immigrants instead of admitting immigrants based on extended family relations. The Commission found no justification for the continued entry of low-skilled foreign nationals.
· End chain migration by allowing immigrants to sponsor only spouses and minor children.
· Prevent the expansion of guest worker programs for low-skilled workers. The Commission found that low-skilled workers have far too few opportunities open to them: "When immigrants are less well-educated and less skilled, they may pose economic hardships for the most vulnerable of Americans."
· Eliminate the Visa Lottery (55,000 immigrant visas awarded randomly every year).
· Scrutinize the basic rules of naturalization. Naturalization should not be an avenue to welfare.

- Give more attention to the integration process and not just admission policies. The Commission found a great need to emphasize Americanization.

Barbara Jordan emphasized the importance of Americanization (assimilation) in the immigration process. She stated: "That word earned a bad reputation when it was stolen by racists and xenophobes in the 1920s. But it is our word, and we are taking it back. "[13]

Impact on American workers was an important consideration. Barbara Jordan stated: "Immigration policy must protect US workers against unfair competition from foreign workers, with an appropriately higher level of protection to the most vulnerable in our society"[14]

Former SEIU Vice President Eliseo Medina served as a member of Obama's National Latino Advisory Council and as honorary chair of the Democratic Socialists of America. At the 2009 America's Future Now! Conference Medina presented a plan for establishing long-term Democrat majorities using blanket amnesty. "We reform the immigration laws; it puts 12 million people on the path to citizenship and eventually voters. If we have eight million new voters who care about, and will be voting, we will be creating a governing coalition for the long term."[15]

Before the 2012 midterms Representative Luis Gutierrez during an interview with MSNBC stated that some in his party could be negatively impacted by a blanket amnesty for undocumented immigrants. Gutierrez then stated:

"Let me just say in about an hour, I'm going over to the White House. I'll be meeting with Jeh Johnson and the Chief Legal Counsel to the President of the United States. We're going to sit down and we're going to negotiate additional terms and avenues the President can use and prosecutorial discretion, and I think we can get three or four or maybe even five million people."[16]

That is four to five million new Democrat voters. Should immigration policy be crafted to be a voter recruitment tool without concern for the interest of the American public? I don't think so. The Jordan Commission presented bi-partisan recommendations in the interest of the nation with concern for the middle class and vulnerable groups. For some time, I questioned if either party in Washington, DC, wanted to solve the problem of illegal immigration. Were the programs simply smoke and mirrors for public consumption? Did the programs serve as political payback for donors? Republican and Democrat politicians have donors to please with illegals willing to work for less suppressing the blue-collar wages.

The Trump administration laid out a whole new direction for illegal immigration. During his State of the Union Speech February 4th, 2020, President Trump made the following claims:

- Since my election, we have created 7 million new jobs—5 million more than government experts projected during the previous administration.

- The unemployment rate is the lowest in over half a century. And very incredibly, the average unemployment rate under my administration is lower than any administration in the history of our country.
- The unemployment rate for African Americans, Hispanic Americans, and Asian Americans has reached the lowest levels in history.
- African American youth unemployment has reached an all-time low. African American poverty has declined to the lowest rate ever recorded.
- The unemployment rate for women reached the lowest level in almost 70 years. And, last year, women filled 72 percent of all new jobs added.
- The veteran's unemployment rate dropped to a record low. The unemployment rate for disabled Americans has reached an all-time low.
- Workers without a high school diploma have achieved the lowest unemployment rate recorded in US history. A record number of young Americans are now employed.
- 7 million Americans have come off food stamps, and 10 million people have been lifted off welfare.
- In just three years of my administration, 3.5 million people—working-age people—have joined the workforce.
- Since my election, the net worth of the bottom half of wage earners has increased by 47 percent—three times faster than the increase for the top 1 percent.
- After decades of flat and falling incomes, wages are

rising fast—and, wonderfully, they are rising fastest for low-income workers, who have seen a 16 percent pay increase since my election.

· This is a blue-collar boom.

· Real median household income is now at the highest level ever recorded

Both CNN and PolitiFact "fact checkers" reluctantly confirmed these claims.[17, 18] So why then did the members of the Congressional Black Caucus (CBC) display the solemnity you could expect at a funeral.[19] Shouldn't they have been excited that things are finally improving in the communities they represent? Unfortunately, politics takes precedent over service to the constituency.

Do our politicians value the poor from other countries more than the poor they have failed to serve in our country for so many generations? Politicians over three administrations, Clinton, Bush and Obama, and numerous congresses, regardless of party control, were willing to spend billions of dollars on border security programs that were not effective. The result of mass illegal immigration has been suppression of wages for blue collar employees and the working poor. So, in 2023 the immigration crisis continues. Now (October 2023) international drug cartels effectively have operational control of the US southern border.[20, 21, 22] Human and sex trafficking is rampant and fentanyl poisonings exceed 100,000 per year.[23]

CHAPTER 11

THE BIG SWITCH— YES, BUT WHY?

I first heard of the political narrative "The Big Switch" in the 1970's. It is true a big switch occurred. The implication was that the racist southern Democrats that switched poisoned the entire Republican barrel. I found this narrative offensive. After all I wasn't sympathetic to the segregationist cause. I'm going to challenge the narrative for why the switch occurred. Very important historical puzzle pieces were ignored for a purely political purpose. This could be an important Red Pill moment.

April 10, 2019 Becky Little updated an earlier posting in history titled: "How the 'Party of Lincoln' Won Over the Once Democratic South."[1] Following is her, and I would say the Democrat party explanation for the switch.

The Republican party was originally founded in the mid-1800s to oppose immigration and the spread of slavery, says David Goldfield, whose new book on American politics, The Gifted Generation: When Government Was Good, comes out in November.

"The Republican party was strictly a sectional party, meaning that it just did not exist in the South," he says. "The South couldn't care less about immigration." But it did care about preserving slavery.

After the Civil War, the Democratic party's opposition to Republican Reconstruction legislation solidified its hold on the South.

"The Democratic party came to be more than a political party in the South—it came to be a defender of a way of life," Goldfield says. "And that way of life was the restoration as much as possible of white supremacy ... The Confederate statues you see all around were primarily erected by Democrats."

Up until the post-World War II period, the party's hold on the region was so entrenched that Southern politicians usually couldn't get elected unless they were Democrats. But when President Harry S. Truman, a Democratic Southerner, introduced a pro-civil rights platform at the party's 1948 convention, a faction walked out.

These defectors, known as the "Dixiecrats," held a separate convention in Birmingham, Alabama. There, they nominated South Carolina Governor Strom Thurmond, a staunch opposer of civil rights, to run for president on their "States' Rights" ticket. Although Thurmond lost the election to Truman, he still won over a million popular votes.

It "was the first time since before the Civil War that the South was not solidly Democratic," Goldfield says. "And that began the erosion of the southern influence in the Democratic party."

After that, the majority of the South still continued to vote Democratic because it thought of the Republican party as the party of Abraham Lincoln and Reconstruction. The big break didn't come until President Johnson, another Southern Democrat, signed the Civil Rights Act in 1964 and the Voting Rights Act in 1965.

Though some Democrats had switched to the Republican party prior to this, "the defections became a flood" after Johnson signed these acts, Goldfield says. "And so the political parties began to reconstitute themselves."

The change wasn't total or immediate. During the late 1960s and early '70s, white Southerners were still transitioning away from the Democratic party (newly enfranchised black Southerners voted and continue to vote Democratic). And even as Republican Richard Nixon employed a "Southern strategy" that appealed to the racism of Southern white voters, former Alabama Governor George Wallace (who'd wanted "segregation now, segregation tomorrow, and segregation forever") ran as a Democrat in the 1972 presidential primaries.

By the time Ronald Reagan became president in 1980, the Republican party's hold on white Southerners was firm. Today, the Republican party remains the party of the South. It's an ironic outcome considering that a century ago, white Southerners would've never considered voting for the party of Lincoln.

I believe the details listed above are factually true though incomplete explanation. However, I was at first puzzled by the statement: *"The Confederate statues you see all around were primarily erected by Democrats."* Why not exclusively by Democrats? One Memorial that came to mind was the Confederate Memorial in Arlington National Cemetery.

This memorial occurred with approval of Republican Administrations to promote national unity. The Arlington National Cemetery web site states:

"In 1898, mobilization for war against Spain, and the United States' expanding global power, reinforced a sense of national unity—at least among many white Americans.

...December 14, 1898—four days after the Spanish-American War ended—President William McKinley kicked off his "Peace Jubilee" nationwide tour with a speech in Atlanta in which he proclaimed, "in the spirit of fraternity we should share with you in the care of the graves of Confederate soldiers.... Sectional feeling no longer holds back the love we feel for each other. The old flag again waves over us in peace with new glories."

...Notably, this 'spirit of fraternity' did not include African Americans.

...In 1906, with Secretary of War William Howard Taft's approval, the United Daughters of the Confederacy (a hereditary organization of Southern women) began raising funds to erect a memorial in the Confederate section...

...On June 7, 1903, the first Confederate Memorial Day ceremonies were held in Arlington's Confederate section. President Theodore Roosevelt sent a floral arrangement, beginning a tradition continued by nearly every US president. In 2009, President Barack Obama modified the tradition, sending two wreaths: one to the Confederate Memorial, the other to Washington, DC's African American Civil War Memorial, in honor of US Colored Troops...

...An inscription of the Latin phrase "Victrix causa diis placuit sed victa Caton" ("The victorious cause was pleasing to the gods, but the lost cause to Cato") construes the South's secession as a noble "Lost Cause." This narrative of the Lost Cause, which romanticized the pre-Civil War South and denied the horrors of slavery...

This Memorial was dedicated in 1914 during the Wilson Administration.[2] The 'Lost Cause" was a theme Wilson embraced in his text "History of the American People." A show of unity during the Jim Crow Progressive Common Era. This is the only Confederate Memorial I'm aware of erected with Republican support. Recall, 1914 was the centennial of the Battle of Baltimore when Francis Scott Key wrote the "The Star-Spangled Banner." This is also when supporters launched a campaign to designate "The Star-Spangled Banner" as the one and only national anthem. The Republican preferences were "The Battle Hymn of the Republic" or "America the Beautiful." Two years later President Woodrow Wilson designated the "Banner" as the national anthem via executive order.

So, what was left out of Becky Little's narrative. On May 24, 2023, Rick Chomey published: "The Big Switch That Wasn't: The Dixiecrats, Race and 1964."[3] Rick documents additional pertinent facts.

CHAPTER 11: THE BIG SWITCH—YES, BUT WHY?

First,

"The Truman Administration—following sixteen years of Franklin D. Roosevelt—further desired to federalize and centralize government. The Southern Thurmond "Dixiecrats" believed in traditional "states' rights" and segregation. The Northern and Western Democratic Party in the 1930s and 1940s was more "progressive" politically. President Roosevelt's fascination with the Italian dictator Benito Mussolini and fascist government programs in Europe guided many of his domestic policies."

Second,

"In fact, most of these racist libertarians returned to the Democratic Party after 1948 and became a significant voting block against civil rights and desegregation throughout the 1950s and early 1960s. According to one historical analysis of the 1500+ racist "Dixiecrats" only Strom Thurmond and about a dozen others left the Democratic Party for the GOP (less than 1 percent). Furthermore, Thurmond didn't switch parties until 16 years after Truman forced his hand to create his "Dixiecrat" party."

Third

"Again, the Democratic Party was moving left, toward socialism, nonreligious/atheism and adopting liberal planks on abortion, women and gay rights. The Bible Belt South in the 1970s and 1980s became less racist as desegregation and civil rights laws were enforced. Consequently, immigration to southern cities (Atlanta, Dallas, Houston, Nashville, Charlotte) by northern and western GOP conservatives rearranged the voting demographic. Southerners are more conservative and that's why dozens of Democrats switched parties. Did you know notable Republicans Trent Lott, Mike Pence, William Bennett and Rick Perry were all previously Democrat? It's true. And race was not the reason they switched affiliations...it was due to liberal/socialist policies."

Passage of the 1964 Civil Rights Act required Republican support as the Democrats controlled both the house and senate. In the Senate 69 percent of Democrats and 82 percent of Republicans voted Yea. In the House 63 percent of Democrats and 80 percent of Republicans voted Yea, The same was true of the 1965 voting rights act. In the Senate 73 percent of Democrats and 94 percent of Republicans voted Yea. In the House 78 percent of Democrats and 83 percent of Republicans voted "yea." Why would the "Dixiecrats" move to the Republican party that supported what they opposed more than their own party?[4, 5]

Senator Robert Byrd had voted Nay on the 1964 Civil Rights act and no vote for the 1965 Voting Rights act. Chromey suggested that Robert Byrd may be an example to consider.

"Byrd spent 62 years in public office. He served for over half a century at the national level, as a Representative and, later, a powerful Senator. The senior senator died in office (2010) at the ripe age of 92. Hillary Clinton called Byrd a 'friend and mentor.' Barack Obama noted how 'the arc of his life bent toward justice.' The press gave Byrd a surprisingly, blessed pass and ignored his racism.

That's because Robert Byrd proved a quintessential post-WW2 Democrat. Originally a member and leader of the Ku Klux Klan in West Virginia (an affiliation he later disavowed), Byrd refused to fight in World War II because it meant serving alongside blacks. He routinely voted with other segregationists in the 1950s. As a senator, Byrd filibustered and voted against the 1964 Civil Rights Act. He abstained his vote for the 1965 Voting Act. He also voted against the confirmation of Thurgood Marshall, the first black Supreme Court justice.

This same Robert Byrd then politically transformed from a known racist to a beloved mentor. How? Simple. He towed the party line...for nearly 57 years! It's possible to argue Byrd didn't lose his racism but rather, like most good politicians, shelved it. He enjoyed his power and position. It wasn't the first time Byrd did what was necessary. In fact, the whole reason Byrd initially joined the KKK was for 'political power.' To his credit, Byrd did leave the organization, but still it showed him to be a political opportunist. Once in national office, at least until 1967 (when being a segregationist went out of fashion), he retained his racist roots. Byrd told a reporter: "Don't get that albatross [the KKK] around your neck. Once you've made that mistake, you inhibit your operations in the political arena.'"

Like Robert Byrd Mississippi Senator James Eastland voted against the 1964 Civil Rights act. He also voted against the 1965 Voting Rights act. Senator Eastland became the powerful head of the Senate Judiciary committee and remained a Democrat until his death in 1981.[6]

Governor George Wallace[7] of Alabama is another interesting case. For his George Wallace was infamous for his segregationist positions. On January 14, 1963, George Wallace was inaugurated governor of Alabama. In his inaugural speech he promised "Segregation now, segregation tomorrow, segregation forever".[8] George Wallace died in 1998 at the age of 79, still a Democrat.

Enough, let's see 1500+ racist "Dixiecrats" and about a dozen leave less than 1 percent. It seems by far the most common method for racist southern democrat politicians to leave the party was to die.

In the antebellum south characteristics of life on the plantation for the slaves included:

- Substandard housing
- Poorly fed
- Poorly clothed
- Poor or no education
- Despair
- Family separation

- Short life span
- Over worked.

All apply in America's cities today except for maybe the last. What big switch I ask?

In the chapter titled Scientific Racism we learned of the past racist transgressions of the Ivy League during the Jim Crow Progressive Common Era. We also discussed how American Eugenists collaborated with their Nazi counterparts. We learned that Planned Parenthood is no longer praising Margret Sanger but distancing themselves from her racist past. It seems like this Big Switch narrative is a myth of convenience. Is it an effort to cover the connections between earlier progressives and the Nazi's? Will the politicians and academics that support the myth ever defend the policies they or their predecessors have promoted?

CHAPTER 12
THE COACH

As a Green Bay Packer fan growing up in the sixties every-body knew what you meant when you said, "The Coach." There have been many great coaches over the last 50-60 years, but when somebody says, "The Coach" they are still referring to Vince Lombardi. The coach challenged his players to be the best people they could be. Some people thought him too harsh but there are so many great quotes that are repeated today. I've always enjoyed a very simple one from a game where his team was not playing their best, Lombardi simply said: "What the hell is going on out here?"[1]

Only with the truth can we dial back social tensions and obtain cultural unity to obtain that more perfect union. In this the age of the internet and alternate media we have an opportunity to expose the truth and come together.

If racism was such a problem in this country in 2019, why did Jussie Smollett have to fake it. Jussie's not alone. I've heard of many instances of fake hate crimes over the years. Furthermore, why would whites pass as black such as Rachel Dolezal.[2] You could call it cultural appropriation for profit and advancement. A great example of that is Senator Elizabeth Warren.[3]

It's a far cry from University of Penn professor Dr. Samuel Morton publishing "Crania Americana" in 1839, the study of craniology where he promoted the idea you could predict a person's character, intelligence and morals from skull characteristics. Or the study of eugenics, imported from England which had much the same hypothesis. Eugenics which informed Ivy League elitists to formally segregate society and justified separate but equal education.

Today many American Universities are adopting neo-segregation. In a study published in 2019 it was found that:

- 46 percent offer segregated orientation programs.
- 43 percent offer segregated housing arrangements.
- 72 percent offer segregated commencement ceremonies.
- ETC...[4]

Will the elites in this nation ever allow the public to get along or will they constantly attempt to divide us? To paraphrase coach Lombardi: "What the hell is going on at America's universities?"

An October 9, 2023, New York Post article was titled: "31 Harvard Student Groups' Despicable Letter Backing Hamas Exposes the Deep Sickness of US Academia."[5] The same day Newsweek released an article titled: "Harvard

Students Blaming Israel for Hamas Attacks Sparks Fury: 'Despicable.'"[6]

These two articles speak to Harvard students but in fact protests occurred at other universities as well.[7] Secretary of State, Anthony Blinken stated October 10, 2023: "Hamas has only one agenda, to destroy Israel and to murder Jews."[8]

As reported previously, during the first half of the 1900s Harvard was promoting the science of eugenics. Harvard and other American academics consulted with the Nazis promoting eugenic development of the "human stock." Today students and faculty at Harvard and other American universities protest in support of an organization that essentially wants to complete Hitler's "Final Solution" which was to annihilate the Jews. I find that extremely disturbing.

As American whites turned from their previous trained/gaslight bigotry, the ruling elite needed some other means to maintain control/power. Again, reflect on my experience described under the subtitle "music tames the savage beast." I believe, as a generation, baby boomers were brought together through our music and the civil rights legislation passed in the '60s. But then the story of the big switch was told and used as a tool to divide and distract from the reality that systemic racism emanates from *government policies* which began during the Jim Crow Progressive Common Era and continue today.

THE GREAT BETRAYAL

As I write today, October 14, 2023, I am shocked at the state of this nation. The USA appears to be on fire. Believe me, both political parties are at fault. Remember the Jim Crow Progressive Common Era included Republicans and Democrats? Since Inauguration Day 2021 we've observed accelerated upheaval in American society and the world. Let's recap. First, average monthly inflation jumped from under 2 percent in 2020 to 4.7 percent in 2021, 8 percent in 2022 and 4.4 percent by September 2023. All due to excess government spending with printed money.[9] At the same time wages are not keeping up with inflation and the public knows it.

Second, illegal border crossings continue to soar as the administration claims they have operational control of the border. Today citizens of New York and Chicago are complaining as it seems the government cares more about the illegal immigrants than the citizens they were elected to serve. Some illegal immigrants turn themselves in but others do not. As reported in the Washington Examiner on August 28, 2023, "Among the more than 8.6 million people who've illegally entered the US since President Joe Biden took office, at least nearly 1.6 million are "gotaways."[10]

The got aways include those trafficking in drugs, guns, or the child and adult sex trade, or other nefarious purposes.

Third, President Biden announced the draw-down of US troops in Afghanistan would be completed by the 20th anniversary of September 11th.[11] Unfortunately, because of the rough implementation of the withdrawal the claims of its great success rang hollow. A report from the Washington Examiner on August 19, 2021, included the following.

"British members of Parliament railed against President Joe Biden on Wednesday, lamenting his chaotic and dishonorable withdrawal from Afghanistan.

The complaints weren't specifically targeted against Biden's decision to withdraw US. forces from Afghanistan. Instead, it was the feckless, unprepared, and callous method of Biden's retreat that has sparked such anger...

Tobias Ellwood observed that it isn't a collapse of Western security forces that we've seen over the past few days, but rather "it's the leadership that is going." Owen Paterson went further, asserting that Britain will "now have to deal with a weak American president." [12]

Today, American interests seem to be challenged on multiple fronts, from the war in Ukraine to China's saber rattling over Taiwan and now Hamas attacks on Israel.

I titled this section The Great Betrayal as I've come to believe that the republic, I thought we lived in was corrupted a long time ago. Between the Civil War and the Progressive Era, the black community had begun to make "social progress" in spite of the great injustices inflicted on it. Teddy Roosevelt welcomed qualified black people into the Federal government. As a nation we were moving closer to the ideals expressed in the preamble to the US constitution.

"We the People of the United States, in Order to form a more perfect Union, establish Justice, ensure domestic Tranquility, provide for the common defence, promote the general Welfare, and secure the Blessings of Liberty to ourselves and our Posterity, do ordain and establish this Constitution for the United States of America."[13]

The early progressives believed in a more powerful administrative state than the founding fathers. TR was a progressive, however, he had limits of fairness he would not cross. Woodrow Wilson expressed the Progressive view of the administrative state as follows.

"All that progressives ask or desire is permission—in an era when 'development,' 'evolution,' is the scientific word—to interpret the Constitution according to the Darwinian principle; all they ask is recognition of the fact that a nation is a living thing and not a machine."

And following Francis Galton's branch of evolutionary thinking, eugenics, society was segregated, hospitals were set up to commit the insane, physically disabled, criminalistic, feebleminded or otherwise "flawed" which could involve forced sterilizations. As history has shown Hitler's Nazis followed suit a few decades latter.

I don't know how this was covered up for so long,

but I would add that many people in the early 1900s had to leave school young to support their families and few attended universities. Perhaps it was forgotten during the misery of the Great Depression. Today we see in real time how the media spins and distorts news. It's clear our universities had motivation to downplay this history. Their business model was to train the "experts" that would run the government and plan society. As mentioned earlier, until the 1960s, with a few limited exceptions, the Ivy League was predominantly an elitest white protestant boys' club that brought considerable social and business connections.

So, who were the elites planning society? Oliver Wendell Holmes Sr. coined the phrase "Boston Brahmin" in an 1861 book in which he described his social class as "a physical and mental elite, identifiable by its noble 'physiognomy' and 'aptitude for learning,'"[14] which he insisted were "congenital and hereditary."

They included some of New England's oldest families dating back to before the American Revolution. And their families are likely around today. The New England Historical society identifies Former Secretary of State John Kerry as a Brahmin by marriage on his mother's side.[15]

Another family with roots back to American Revolution is the Bush family. Captain Timothy Bush Sr. was a militia captain during the Revolutionary War. He was also the great- great- great- great- great-grandfather to George H W Bush.[16] His wife Barbara had deep family roots as well.[17]

New York had "the four hundred" which, due to

CHAPTER 12: THE COACH

Ward McAllister, would possibly bring in some of the ex-confederate crowd as well as New York's old money.

I mention these connections as a point of historical interest. I've heard on several occasions of old money interest working in the background quietly influencing society. It is my intent to focus on more recent developments.

About 1980, I read an article in a national magazine, Scientific American or Smithsonian or some other, I'm not sure which. I found the article disturbing as it promoted the idea that the United States would become the manager of information for the world. This was more than a decade before I became aware of the internet in the early 1990s. The article further predicted that manufacturing would move overseas helping raise living standards for other parts of the world. I found this prospect very disturbing on two counts. First, where would people working blue collar jobs find employment? It seemed to me the standard of living for blue collar employees would be drastically reduced if employed at all. Secondly, I firmly believed that to have a strong national economy you had to control production, not offshore production.

During the early 1990s I was the lead mechanical engineer for a team developing a new, novel power electronics product line for the Westinghouse Electric Corporation. The management team agreed we should maximize domestic hardware content as much as possible. At that time, the corporate name of Westinghouse still commanded respect in American industry. When I would call suppliers for fasteners, fans, connectors, etc., sales representatives were always extremely interested in our product and what our expectations were for sales. During these discussions I frequently got insight into the challenges domestic manufacturers were facing from foreign competition. I found this genuinely concerning.

During the early to mid-1990s my family had a subscription to the Washington Post. About this time, I read an article describing the contracts American companies had to sign to set up manufacturing in China. As would be expected the company would finance the factory and train the staff and factory employees. To my surprise companies were also required to establish centers to train engineers to design the products. The last stipulation I recall was that the company would not be allowed to sell more than 25 percent of their production in China. The argument given for companies offshoring to China was simple. China was a massive untapped, underdeveloped market and the USA and European manufacturers there would have greater efficiency. The obvious conclusion was that this is the transferring of whole industries from the USA and Europe to China, and a major betrayal of working-class, blue-collar citizens.

Additionally, China promised a relaxed regulatory environment reducing cost while the United States regulatory agencies continued to burden domestic manufacturers with more stringent demands. I remember thinking the totalitarian communist country was allowing our manufacturers more freedom than our own government, at the same time the "free world" was placing more controls on business. That was a head scratcher. Now in 2023 we are concerned with supply chain problems as many of the goods we consume are getting stuck in transit. Does that make any sense?

A case in point was when President Biden signed the Chips Act into law in August of 2022. The president referred to this act as "a once in a generation investment in America itself." The act authorized $53 billion dollars in subsidies to support research and development for American semi-conductor manufacturers. Domestic manufacturers have promised investments of their own. Microchips/semiconductors are found in household items from cell phones to coffee pots and microwaves as well as cars. Additionally, they are critical to our nation's defense.[18]

This technology was invented in the US in the late '50s and early '60s.[19] As a young boy I could listen to my favorite music on my AM transistor radio, outside even. Yes AM! That's as good as it got back then. In 1990 the US produced 37 percent of the world's chips however US production had dropped to 12 percent by the time the legislation was signed.[20] The question I had in the 1990s was why US politicians didn't adjust policies to stem the flow of American jobs/production offshore. The answer comes down to pure greed on the part of "elites" in American society including members of both political parties or should we say the "Uniparty." I see this as a problem that began slowly in the 1970s but really ramped up in the 1990s.

Peter Schweizer's 2022 book "Red Handed" documents how the American public has been sold out. The book jacket includes the following statement: "Presidential families, Silicon Valley Gurus, Wall Street high rollers, Ivy League universities, even professional athletes–all are willing to sacrifice American strength and security on the altar of personal enrichment."

A complete list of those referenced includes current and former Senators and Representatives or family members as well as former Secretaries of State, defense and intelligence officials from both political parties.[21] These people influenced federal and state policy in a manner that benefited Chinese interests. The jacket text states "Presidential families," and Schweizer lists Bush family members as well as the Bidens.

A March 31, 2022 article in Newsweek by Wells King tells a very damming story. The article is titled "Globalization: America's Biggest Bipartisan Mistake/Opinion"[22] Following are some selections from the article.

"For more than two decades, a bipartisan collection of politicians, academics, business leaders and policy 'experts'—call them the 'Uniparty'—devoted much of its energy to fighting for, and later defending, an unquestioning commitment to the free flow of people, goods and capital around the world."

"As President George W. Bush argued, 'Societies that open to commerce will one day open to liberty.' It was an inevitability: the possibility that nations like China might adopt one but not the other was not, therefore, a matter of concern."

"And besides," argued Clinton treasury secretary Larry Summers, "welcoming China into the global economic system is right for the American economy and for the global economy."

"President Bill Clinton insisted 'globalization is not something that we can hold off or turn off. It is the economic equivalent of a force of nature.'"

"The Uniparty's promise never panned out, and free trade failed to free the world from authoritarianism—look no further than the Chinese Communist Party. But America still paid the price of unfair competition and offshoring."

For some time, I have been questioning why the public is constantly receiving promises that Washington, DC, doesn't keep. Why does the average citizen feel they are falling behind? Do the members of the "Uniparty" feel the same way? I suspect not. I feel as though we, the public, are being manipulated and pitted against one another. It's as though the system is "rigged" so the "elite" and influential win at everyone else's expense. Do they protect their own? Would they turn on someone or persons who potentially or literally exposed "Uniparty" malfeasance?

The following is a possible example of just such a case. An example of an extremely popular entertainer who, if the charges against him are true, had been protected by the "elites" of society.

The NAACP staged a gala celebration in Washington, DC, on May 17th, 2004 to celebrate the Brown v Board of

Education decision against school segregation. Bill Cosby, beloved comedian, actor, and philanthropist was asked to deliver the main address. Cosby took the occasion to deliver a highly critical critique of shortcomings in the black community. That speech is known as the "Pound Cake" speech.

Following are some excerpts from the speech.

"Ladies and gentlemen, I really have to ask you to seriously consider what you've heard, and now this is the end of the evening so to speak. I heard a prize fight manager say to his fellow who was losing badly, 'David, listen to me. It's not what's he's doing to you. It's what you're not doing.'"

"Ladies and gentlemen, these people set (civil rights leaders of the 1950s and 1960s)—they opened the doors, they gave us the right, and today, ladies and gentlemen, in our cities and public schools we have 50 percent drop out. In our own neighborhood, we have men in prison. No longer is a person embarrassed because they're preg-nant without a husband. No longer is a boy considered an embarrassment if he tries to run away from being the father of the unmarried child. Ladies and gentlemen, the lower economic and lower middle economic people are not holding their end in this deal. In the neighborhood that most of us grew up in, parenting is not going on. In the old days, you couldn't hooky school because every drawn shade was an eye. And before your mother got off the bus and to the house, she knew exactly where you had gone, who had gone into the house, and where you got on whatever you had on and where you got it from. Parents don't know that today..."[23, 24]

For his speech Cosby received a firestorm of protest and blow back. However, Cosby did not back down. He made the following comments in the months to come:

"It makes no sense to claim that these are things that belong quietly in the black community. We have to figure out how do you get parenting back into the home. This is a problem of epic proportion."

"I think that it is time for concerned African-Americans to march, galvanize and raise the awareness about this epidemic, to transform our helplessness, frustration, and righteous indignation into a sense of shared responsibility and action."

"I feel that I can no longer remain silent. If I have to make a choice between keeping quiet so that conservative media does not speak negatively or ringing the bell to galvanize those who want change in the lower economic community, then I choose to be a bell ringer."

"You've got to stop beating up your women because you can't find a job, because you didn't want to get an education and now you're (earning) minimum wage. You should have thought more of yourself when you were in high school, when you had an opportunity."[25]

Over the years since upwards of 60 women accused Cosby of drugging and/or assault. For most of the accusations the statute of limitations had already run out. Cosby has repeatedly denied all accusations. One accuser, Andrea Constand, had made accusations against Cosby in January 2005 regarding an incident in 2004.[26] However, Montgomery County District Attorney Bruce Castor stated that *he* "finds insufficient, credible, and admissible evidence exists upon which any charge against Mr. Cosby could be sustained beyond a reasonable doubt."

In 2015 Cosby was in court on the same charge. He was ultimately convicted in 2018 and the conviction subsequently overturned on legal technicalities.[27] It is not my intent to pass judgement on this case. I am questioning if Cosby was protected for decades by "elites" who dominate society.

I believe Cosby was right to challenge the black community. In education, as in athletics, if you don't practice you won't be prepared for the game of life. However, he should have also challenged the public officials who keep these communities trapped in perpetually failing public schools. For decades these communities have asked for school choice. Let the dollars follow the student not trap the student in the failing school. But then that would impact the power of the teachers' unions and resultant donations to politicians. I for one believe Jeffrey Epstein and Harvey Weinstein were protected for years until it was more convenient to dump them.

CHAPTER 12: THE COACH

THE GRUBERIZATION OF A NATION

How does the government manipulate the public? Here's one example. In 2013 MIT Economist and Architect of Obamacare, Johnathan Gruber said,

"In terms of risk-rated subsidies, if you had a law which said that healthy people are going to pay in—you made explicit that healthy people pay in and sick people get money, it would not have passed, okay. **Lack of transparency is a huge political advantage.** And basically, call it the stupidity of the American voter or whatever, but basically that was really, really critical for the thing to pass... Look, I wish Mark was right that we could make it all transparent, but I'd rather have this law than not."[28, 29, 30, 31]

"...[A] lack of transparency is a powerful political tool..." so we're speaking of legislative and publicity sleight of hand misrepresenting what the legislation will do. And who are they deceiving but those who support the legislation? Those who opposed this legislation were not the target of the deception.

While in Nazi prison during WWII Dietrich Bonhoeffer wrote his "Theory on Stupidity." I should add, Bonhoeffer is speaking of Germans who adopted the narrative of the German National Socialist Workers party, the Nazis. Bonhoeffer believed that very intelligent people under the pressure of political power and propaganda were rendered stupid, incapable of critical thinking.

"Stupidity is a more dangerous enemy of the good than wickedness. Evil can be protested against, exposed, and, if necessary, it can be prevented by force. Evil always harbors the germ of self-destruction by inducing at least some uneasiness in people. We are defenseless against stupidity. Nothing can be done to oppose it, neither with protests nor with violence. Reasons cannot prevail. Facts that contradict one's prejudice simply don't need to be believed, and when they are inescapable, they can simply be brushed aside as meaningless, isolated cases.

In contrast to evil, the stupid person is completely satisfied with himself. When irritated, he becomes dangerous and may even go on the attack. More caution is therefore required when dealing with the stupid than with the wicked. Never try to convince the stupid with reasons; it's pointless and dangerous.

To understand how to deal with stupidity, we must try to understand its nature. This much is certain: it is not essentially an intellectual, but a human defect. There are people who are intellectually agile who are stupid, while intellectually inept people may be anything but stupid. We discover this to our surprise in certain situations.

One gets the impression that stupidity is often not an innate defect, but one that emerges under certain circumstances in which people are made stupid or allow themselves to be made stupid. We also observe that isolated and solitary people exhibit this defect less frequently than socializing groups of people. Thus, perhaps stupidity is less a psychological than a sociological problem. It is a special manifestation of the influence of historical circumstances on man—a psychological side effect of certain external conditions..." Dietrich Bonhoeffer[32, 33]

LET'S BRING THIS HOME

Earlier Wells King referred to the "Uniparty;" another appropriate term would be "the swamp." Whatever you call them, they appear to be profiting from their public responsibilities while the citizenry does not. In order to continue their cash flow, the "Uniparty" must keep the citizenry fighting, in a constant state of tension.

As I write this the national debt is 33.6 trillion dollars and rising rapidly.[34] Yet for the last 30 years we've been told America's infrastructure is crumbling. It is reported that 45,000 bridges are structurally deficient.[35] When a new report gives the American education system a failing grade the answer is more money. But there never seems to be any improvement and never change of approach. Why have we been in perpetual war for the last 20+ years. Is somebody getting rich with all this spending? Not me, that's for sure. But people in the Uniparty appear to be working hard to satisfy their greed.

In his "Theory of Stupidity" Bonhoeffer was speaking of those Germans who accepted the narrative of the National Socialist German Workers Party. In this instance the deception was imposed rapidly in a time of social and economic instability after WWI. After WWII the US was the major economic power untouched by the destruction of the war. As a nation we entered a period of great prosperity.

It was also a time when the "elites" hid connections of the Jim Crow Progressives and Nazi Eugenists. The discriminatory practices of the federal government from Woodrow Wilson on were also covered up. If the public were to realize the federal government and Ivy League, along with other universities, not just the south was responsible for racial segregation, the politicians and academicians of the day would have lost credibility.

Woodrow Wilson, our Jim Crow Progressive president, took a very hardline with people who spoke against America's entrance into WWI. That's where the "evolutionary" view of the Constitution comes in. Did Wilson evolve and change the constitution to whatever he wanted it to be? I think so.

On May 22, 2013, Nick Gillespie published an article in the Daily Beast titled "Obama's War on Journalism: 'An Unconstitutional Act'". The article began with the following paragraph.

> "The press-punishing, speech-chilling, and unabashedly overreaching actions by the Obama administration against the Associated Press and Fox News Channel's James Rosen lay bare the essential dynamic between any president and a press that is always more prone to being lapdogs than watchdogs: the president feeds or punishes them as he sees fit, while chanting a bogus rosary about 'national security.'"

CHAPTER 12: THE COACH

The article describes how the Obama Administration secretly spied on journalists suppressing freedom of the press.[36]

On March 31, 2022, Jill Colvyn published an article on the AP titled "DNC, Clinton campaign agree to Steele dossier funding fine."

The article documents how the Clinton campaign and the DNC had established a tortured path for funding to develop opposition research against the Trump Campaign for the 2016 election. The actions resulted in the now discredited Steele dossier compiled by a former British spy. The dossier was intended to influence the outcome of the 2016 election. The FBI used the dossier to spy on Trump and associates prior to the 2017 inauguration.[37] The investigation resulted in two years of reporting on the progress of the Muller probe which greatly divide the public. The Muller probe was in fact initiated on "disinformation".

But that did not stop the government from election interference as shown in the Twitter files. While 51 former intelligence officers claimed the Hunter Biden laptop story looked like Russian disinformation, a 2022 poll indicates 79 percent of Americans who've been following the Hunter Biden laptop scandal believe that "truthful" coverage would have changed the outcome of the 2020 presidential election.[38] Now we know from testimony before the House that former acting CIA director under President Obama had solicited the Hunter Biden laptop letter at the instigation of Anthony Blinken, a foreign policy advisor to the Biden 2020 campaign.[39] Blinken is now President

Biden's Secretary of State. It appears that in addition to money many in Washington, DC, also want power and are resistant to democratic change.

I've come to believe the American public in our general prosperity had been lulled to sleep after WWII. The constant threat of nuclear war during the cold war kept the public distracted. Recently, we were made to fear the Russians and were not watching what our own government was doing to us. By dividing the public, the "Elites", the "Uniparty," have been able to abuse us without being found out. Bonhoeffer's theory applies to us in that we've been manipulated into two alternate realities. One reality that says the left is evil the other says the right is. They can't both be right. I would suggest both are wrong and that we've all been deceived. That is not to say there isn't significant disagreement as to what should be done. There is, but hopefully we can begin movement toward resolution with civil and rational discussions.

The Coach did not just speak these words he lived them. As defensive lineman and team captain Willie Davis stated: "I would say that nobody had more impact in creating diversity in the NFL than Coach Lombardi. It was partly because he took a new approach, almost playing ignorant to any kind of racial tension in the league."[40] He also supported defensive lineman Lionel Aldridge's desire to marry his white fiancée when interracial marriage wasn't socially acceptable.[41, 42] But then Coach Lombardi would have experienced the bigotry projected toward Italian Americans by the Eugenic elites, Ivy League and others. Coach Lombardi was known as a demanding coach expressed as: "Winning isn't everything but it's the only thing, in our business there is no second place either you're first or you'rer last."[43] A philosophy tempered in his later years: "If you go out on a football field on Sunday, or any endeavor in life and you leave every fiber of what you have on that field when the game finally ends, then you've won... and I never made that clear."[44]

I believe coach Vince Lombardi had the right idea so many years ago: "People who work together will win, whether it be against complex football defenses, or the problems of modern society."[45]

As for me, I've looked at a lot of information and given my interpretation. I do intend to search for more puzzle pieces to fill in the story of US. I hope you'll join me in my quest, there is so much more to explore. If you need to, take the red pill and let's get started. I'm taking a brief break, I'm feeling as mad as a hatter, then back down the rabbit hole.

"... And what does the Lord require
of you but to do justice,
and to love kindness, and to walk humbly
with your God?"
Micah 6:8[46]

NOTES

INTRODUCTION

1. Wikipedia, s.v. "Roger Clemens," last modified June 23, 2024, 17:55, https://en.wikipedia.org/wiki/Roger_Clemens.

2. *Merriam-Webster*, s.v. "gaslight (n.)," https://www.merriam-webster.com/dictionary/gaslight.

3. Marissa Conrad, "What Is Gaslighting? Examples And How To Deal With It," *Forbes Health*, May 15, 2024, https://www.forbes.com/health/mind/what-is-gaslighting/.

4. "The Matrix – Tumbling down the rabbit hole . . .," sprish, April 1, 2009, https://www.youtube.com/watch?app=desktop&v=TbYirSio8m4.

5. "The Matrix – Tumbling down the rabbit hole . . .," sprish, April 1, 2009, https://www.youtube.com/watch?app=desktop&v=TbYirSio8m4.

CHAPTER 1: THE RULING ELITE

1. "Sitting Bull's Story of the Battle," Astonisher, https://www.astonisher.com/archives/museum/sitting_bull_little_big_horn.html.

2. Genevieve Carlton, PhD, "A History of the Ivy League," BestColleges, March 21, 2023, https://www.bestcolleges.com /blog/history-of-ivy-league/.

3. "Theodore Roosevelt," History, November 13, 2009, https:// www.history.com/topics/us-presidents/theodore-roosevelt.

4. Wikipedia, s.v. "Theodore Roosevelt," last modified June 24, 2024, 13:29, https://en.wikipedia.org/wiki/Theodore_Roosevelt.

5. Andrew Duppstadt, "James Iredell Waddell," North Carolina History Project, https://northcarolinahistory.org/encyclopedia /james-iredell-waddell-1824-1886/.

6. Wikipedia, s.v. "Martha Bulloch Roosevelt," last modified April 16, 2024, https://en.wikipedia.org/wiki/Martha_Bulloch _Roosevelt.

7. *The Gilded Age*, created by Julian Fellowes, featuring Carrie Coon, Morgan Spector, and Louisa Jacobson, aired 2022, https:// www.imdb.com/title/tt4406178/.

8. Wikipedia, s.v. "Ward McAllister," last modified February 10, 2024, 15:22, https://en.wikipedia.org/wiki/Ward_McAllister.

9. Britannica, T. Editors of Encyclopaedia, s.v. "Ward McAllister," *Encyclopedia Britannica*, March 22, 2024, https:// www.britannica.com/biography/Ward-McAllister.

10. Wikipedia, s.v. "Varina Anne Davis," last modified May 28, 2024, 16:42, https://en.wikipedia.org/wiki/Varina_Anne _Davis.

11. "Varina Davis," *History of American Women* (blog), https://www.womenhistoryblog.com/2010/06/varina-davis.html.

12. Encyclopedia Virigina Staff, s.v. "Varina David (1826-1906)," *Encyclopedia Virginia*, December 7, 2020 https:// encyclopediavirginia.org/entries/davis-varina-1826-1906/.

13. Wikipedia, s.v. "Sara Agnes Rice Pryor," last modified May 10, 2024, 19:56, https://en.wikipedia.org/wiki/Sara_Agnes_Rice_Pryor.

14. "The Ku Klux Klan, A Secret History," *The History Channel*, 1998.

CHAPTER 2: SLAVERY AND A NEW NATION

1. Abraham Lincoln, *The Wit and Wisdom of Abraham Lincoln, A Book of Quotations*, (Mineola: Dover Publications, Inc., 2005), 26.

2. Peter Partoll, "The Native Americans Who Owned Slaves," Intellectual Takeout, June 12, 2023, https://intellectualtakeout.org/2023/06/native-americans-owned-slaves/.

3. Wikipedia, s.v. "Amerindian slave ownership," last modified June 5, 2024, 00:25, https://en.wikipedia.org/wiki/Amerindian_slave_ownership.

4. "Native Americans and Slavery," Gale Library of Daily Life: Slavery in America, *Encyclopedia.com*, June 14, 2024, https://www.encyclopedia.com/humanities/applied-and-social-sciences-magazines/native-americans-and-slavery.

5. Peter Partoll, "The Native Americans Who Owned Slaves," Intellectual Takeout, June 12, 2023, https://intellectualtakeout.org/2023/06/native-americans-owned-slaves/.

6. Peter Partoll, "The Native Americans Who Owned Slaves," Intellectual Takeout, June 12, 2023, https://intellectualtakeout.org/2023/06/native-americans-owned-slaves/.

7. History.com Editors, "Writing of Declaration of Independence," History.com, June 22, 2023, https://www.history.com/topics/american-revolution/writing-of-declaration-of-independence.

8. Yohuru Williams, "Why Thomas Jeffersons' Anti-Slavery Passage Was Removed from the Declaration of Independence," History.com, June 26, 2023, https://www.history.com/news/declaration-of-independence-deleted-anti-slavery-clause-jefferson.

9. "King George's Rebellion Proclamation August 23, 1775," Revolutionary War and Beyond, https://www.revolutionary-war-and-beyond.com/king-george-rebellion-proclamation.html.

10. "Why Thomas Jeffersons' Anti-Slavery Passage Was removed from the Declaration of Independence," History News Network, June 29, 2020, https://www.historynewsnetwork.org/article/why-thomas-jeffersons-anti-slavery-passage-was-rem.

11. "Who said this quote We must all hang together or we shall all hang separately?" Wise-Answer, July 5, 2020, https://wise-answer.com/who-said-this-quote-we-must-all-hang-together-or-we-shall-all-hang-separately/.

12. "Loyalists vs Patriots: America's Revolutionary Divide," History in Charts, November 25, 2020, https://historyincharts.com/patriot-and-loyalist-support-for-the-american-revolution/.

13. History.com Editors, "Articles of Confederation," History.com, August 15, 2023, https://www.history.com/topics/early-us/articles-of-confederation.

14. Ed Crews, "Voting in Early America," *Colonial Williamsburg Journal*, Spring 2007, https://research.colonialwilliamsburg.org/Foundation/journal/Spring07/elections.cfm.

15. The Editors of Encyclopaedia Britannica. "George Wythe." *Encyclopedia Britannica*, June 4, 2024. https://www.britannica.com/biography/George-Wythe.

NOTES

16. Wikipedia, s.v. "George Wythe," last modified April 30, 2024, 16:42, https://en.wikipedia.org/wiki/George_Wythe.

17. Wikipedia, s.v. "George Wythe," last modified April 30, 2024, 16:42, https://en.wikipedia.org/wiki/George_Wythe.

18. History.com Editors, "Enlightenment," History.com, February 21, 2020, https://www.history.com/topics/european -history/enlightenment.

19. Rev. William B. Lawrence, "Slavery and the founders of Methodism," UM News, August 13, 2020, https://www.umnews .org/en/news/slavery-and-the-founders-of-methodism.

20. History.com Editors, "Great Awakening," History.com, September 20, 2019, https://www.history.com/topics/european -history/great-awakening.

21. Barbara O'Brien, "When U.S. Christian Denominations Split Over Slavery," Patheos, January 22, 2023, https://www .patheos.com/blogs/thereligioushistorynerd/2023/01/when-u-s -christian-denominations-split-over-slavery/.

22. "Thomas Sowell on slavery and civilization," Thomas SowellTV, February 4, 2021, https://www.youtube.com/watch? app=desktop&v=_BWIZYkIxUg&list=PLOpJiy5R9WMXHgWck2o QL56TCuCjjkuuo&index=6.

23. Thomas Sowell, *Black Rednecks & White Liberals*, (New York: Encounter Books, 2005).

24. "The Fact About Founding Fathers Owning Slaves," Thomas Sowell, February 26, 20203, https://www.youtube.com /watch?app=desktop&v=-EDHEq7-vck.

25. Thomas Sowell, *Black Rednecks & White Liberals*, (New York: Encounter Books, 2005).

26. "Debt," The Jefferson Monticello, https://www

.monticello.org/research-education/thomas-jefferson-encyclo
pedia/debt/.

27. Thomas Sowell, "The truth about John Randolph
owning slaves," February 4, 2021, https://www.youtube.com
/watch?v=8rB8m28pQTw&list=PLOpJiy5R9WMXHgWck2o
QL56TCuCjjkuuo&index=8.

28. Thomas Sowell, *Black Rednecks & White Liberals*, (New
York: Encounter Books, 2005).

29. Thomas Sowell, "The truth about John Randolph
owning slaves," February 4, 2021, https://www.youtube.com
/watch?v=8rB8m28pQTw&list=PLOpJiy5R9WMXHgWck2o
QL56TCuCjjkuuo&index=8.

30. Thomas Sowell, *Black Rednecks & White Liberals*, (New
York: Encounter Books, 2005).

31. Thomas Sowell, "The End Of Slavery Explained –
Full Compilation," July 19, 2021, https://www.youtube.com
/watch?v=mVyM47hOdLE&list=PLOpJiy5R9WMXHgWck2o
QL56TCuCjjkuuo.

32. "The Fact About Founding Fathers Owning Slaves,"
Thomas Sowell, February 26, 20203, https://www.youtube.com
/watch?app=desktop&v=-EDHEq7-vck.

33. Wikipedia, s.v. "George Washington," last modified June
24, 2024, 15:11, https://en.wikipedia.org/wiki/George_Washington.

34. Wikipedia, "Thomas Jefferson," last modified June 26,
2024, 13:56, https://en.wikipedia.org/wiki/Thomas_Jefferson.

35. Thomas Sowell, "The End Of Slavery Explained –
Full Compilation," July 19, 2021, https://www.youtube.com
/watch?v=mVyM47hOdLE&list=PLOpJiy5R9WMXHgWck2o
QL56TCuCjjkuuo.

36. "Gowan Pamphlet," Colonial Williamsburg, https://www.colonialwilliamsburg.org/explore/nation-builders/gowan-pamphlet/.

37. U.S. Const. art. I, § 2, cl. 3.

38. History.com Editors, "Articles of Confederation," August 15, 2023, https://www.history.com/topics/early-us/articles-of-confederation.

39. "The Three-Fifths Clause of the United States Constitution (1787)," https://www.blackpast.org/african-american-history/events-african-american-history/three-fifths-clause-united-states-constitution-1787/.

40. Jake Macaulay, "The Constitution's 3/5 clause agrees, black lives matter," News With Views, July 17, 2016, https://newswithviews.com/the-constitutions-35-clause-agrees-black-lives-matter/.

41. History.com Editors, "Articles of Confederation," August 15, 2023, https://www.history.com/topics/early-us/articles-of-confederation.

42. The Editors of Encyclopaedia Britannica, "Three-fifths compromise," *Encyclopedia Britannica*, January 2, 2023, https://www.britannica.com/topic/state-sovereign-political-entity.

43. Paul Finkelman, "The Union Wasn't Worth the Three-Fifths Compromise on Slavery," *The New York Times*, February 27, 2013, https://www.nytimes.com/roomfordebate/2013/02/26/the-constitutions-immoral-compromise/the-union-wasnt-worth-the-three-fifths-compromise-on-slavery.

44. The Editors of Encyclopaedia Britannica, "Northwest Ordinances," *Encyclopedia Britannica*, April 16, 2024, https://www.britannica.com/event/Northwest-Ordinances.

45. "Missouri Compromise," Historynet.com, https://www.historynet.com/missouri-compromise/.

46. David Tucker, ed., "Speech to Congress about the Tallmadge Amendment," Teaching American History, https://teachingamericanhistory.org/document/speech-to-congress-2/.

47. "Missouri Compromise," Historynet.com, https://www.historynet.com/missouri-compromise/.

48. James Tallmadge Jr., "Here will I hold my stand," https://riverlinkferry.org/according-to-the-tallmadge-amendment.

49. The Editors of Encyclopaedia Britannica, "Missouri Compromise," *Encyclopedia Britannica*, June 20, 2024, https://www.britannica.com/event/Missouri-Compromise.

50. History.com Editors, "Democratic Party," History.com, January 20, 2021, https://www.history.com/topics/us-government-and-politics/democratic-party.

51. History.com Editors, "Mexican – American War," History.com, August 10, 2022, https://www.history.com/topics/19th-century/mexican-american-war#causes-of-the-mexican-american-war.

52. Matthew Jones, "The Wilmot Proviso: Definition, Date, and Purpose," History Cooperative, October 10, 2023, https://historycooperative.org/wilmot-proviso/.

53. "WILMOT, David," History, Art & Archives, U.S. House of Representatives, June 26, 2024, https://history.house.gov/People/Listing/W/WILMOT,-David-(W000566)/.

54. History.com Editors, "Dred Scott Case," History.com, April 25, 2023, https://www.history.com/topics/black-history/dred-scott-case.

55. Wikipedia, s.v. "Roger B. Taney," last modified May 31, 2024, 16:01, https://en.wikipedia.org/wiki/Roger_B._Taney.

56. Abraham Lincoln, *The Wit and Wisdom of Abraham Lincoln, A Book of Quotations*, (Mineola: Dover Publications, Inc., 2005), 51.

57. History.com Editors, "Compromise of 1850," History .com, August 21, 2023, https://www.history.com/topics/slavery /compromise-of-1850.

58. "John Brown Quotes," AZ Quotes, https://www.azquotes .com/author/24386-John_Brown.

59. History.com Editors, "Bleeding Kansas," History.com, April 7, 2021, https://www.history.com/topics/19th-century /bleeding-kansas.

60. National Archives, s.v. "Kansas-Nebraska Act (1854)," last reviewed June 14, 2024, https://www.archives.gov/milestone -documents/kansas-nebraska-act#page-header.

61. "The Little White School House," Ripon Historical Society, https://riponhistory.org/the-little-white-school-house/.

62. "Republican Philadelphia," USHistory.org, https://www .ushistory.org/gop/origins.htm.

63. "Uncle Tom's Cabin," Historynet.com, https://www .historynet.com/uncle-toms-cabin/.

64. "A Moral Battle Cry For Freedom," Harriet Beecher Stowe Center, https://www.harrietbeecherstowecenter.org /harriet-beecher-stowe/uncle-toms-cabin/.

65. "Uncle Tom's Cabin," Historynet.com, https://www .historynet.com/uncle-toms-cabin/.

66. Harriet Beecher Stowe, *Uncle Tom's Cabin*, (Boston: John P. Jewett and Company, 1852).

67. Wikipedia, s.v. "Battle Hymn of the Republic," last modified June 11, 2024, 03:41, https://en.wikipedia.org/wiki /Battle_Hymn_of_the_Republic.

68. Julia Ward Howe, "Battle-Hymn of the Republic," Poetry Foundation, https://www.poetryfoundation.org/poems/44420 /battle-hymn-of-the-republic.

CHAPTER 3: THE CIVIL WAR AND RECONSTRUCTION

1. "Election of 1860," National Park Service, https://www .nps.gov/subjects/inauguration/election-of-1860.htm.

2. Wikipedia, s.v. "1860 United States presidential election," last modified June 21, 2024, 02:39, https://en.wikipedia .org/wiki/1860_United_States_presidential_election.

3. "Election of 1860," National Park Service, https://www .nps.gov/subjects/inauguration/election-of-1860.htm.

4. Bryan Pollard, "How the US Civil War Divided Indian Nations," History.com, July 12, 2023, https://www.history.com /news/civil-war-native-american-indian-territory-cherokee -home-guard.

5. Wikipedia, s.v. "Jefferson Davis," last modified June 25, 2024, 02:22, https://en.wikipedia.org/wiki/Jefferson_Davis.

6. "Stand Watie," American Battlefield Trust, https://www .battlefields.org/learn/biographies/stand-watie.

7. Crusader1307, "CSS 'Shenandoah,'" Stronghold Nation, https://www.stronghold-nation.com/history/ref/css-shenandoah.

8. "CSS Shenendoah learns the war is over," History.com, https://www.history.com/this-day-in-history/css-shenandoah -learns-the-war-is-over.

9. Wikipedia, s.v. "Irvine Bulloch," last modified December 29, 2023, 01:03, https://en.wikipedia.org/wiki/Irvine_Bulloch.

10. Bret Baier, *To Rescue the Republic: Ulysses S. Grant, the Fragile Union, and the Crisis of 1876*, (New York: Mariner Books, 2021), 230.

11. Bret Baier, *To Rescue the Republic: Ulysses S. Grant, the Fragile Union, and the Crisis of 1876*, (New York: Mariner Books, 2021), 265.

12. Bret Baier, *To Rescue the Republic: Ulysses S. Grant, the Fragile Union, and the Crisis of 1876*, (New York: Mariner Books, 2021), 283.

13. Wikipedia, s.v. "Woodrow Wilson and race," last modified June 13, 2024, 03:30, https://en.wikipedia.org/wiki/Woodrow_Wilson_and_race.

14. "The Fact About Founding Fathers Owning Slaves," Thomas Sowell, February 26, 20203, https://www.youtube.com/watch?app=desktop&v=-EDHEq7-vck.

15. "Debt," The Jefferson Monticello, https://www.monticello.org/research-education/thomas-jefferson-encyclopedia/debt/.

CHAPTER 4: SYSTEMIC RACISM

1. Larry Aldelman, "Race the power of an illusion Documentary," California Newsreel.

2. "Samuel George Morton," Penn and Slavery Project, https://pennandslaveryproject.org/exhibits/show/medschool/southerndoctors/samuelmorton.

3. Wikipedia, s.v. "Samuel George Morton," last modified May 28, 2024, 10:55, https://en.wikipedia.org/wiki/Samuel_George_Morton.

4. "A History of Craniology in Race Science and Physical Anthropology," Penn Museum, https://www.penn.museum/sites/morton/craniology.php.

5. "Medical Professors and Graduates," Penn and Slaver Project, https://pennandslaveryproject.org/exhibits/show/medschool/southerndoctors.

6. Wikipedia, "On the Origin of Species," last modified June 16, 2024, 22:18, https://en.wikipedia.org/wiki/On_the _Origin_of_Species.

7. The Editors of Encyclopaedia Britannica, "Francis Galton," *Encyclopedia Britannica*, June 13, 2024, https://www .britannica.com/biography/Francis-Galton.

8. The Editors of Encyclopaedia Britannica, "Francis Galton," *Encyclopedia Britannica*, June 13, 2024, https://www .britannica.com/biography/Francis-Galton.

9. The Editors of Encyclopaedia Britannica, "Francis Galton," *Encyclopedia Britannica*, June 13, 2024, https://www .britannica.com/biography/Francis-Galton.

10. "Maafa 21 – Black Genocide in 21st Century America – fully documentary," Live Action, Febuary 22, 2018, https://www .youtube.com/watch?v=I6XfU8KVkzI.

11. History.com Editors, "Theodore Roosevelt," History.com, February 7, 2024, https://www.history.com/topics/us-presidents /theodore-roosevelt.

12. Deborah Davis, *Guest of Honor, Booker T Washington, Theodore Roosevelt, and the White House Dinner That Shocked a Nation*, (New York: ATRIA Books, 2012).

13. Larry Aldelman, "Race the power of an illusion Documentary," California Newsreel.

14. Christopher Klein, "How Teddy Roosevelt's Belief in a Racial Hierarchy Shaped His Policies," History.com, August 24, 2023, https://www.history.com/news/teddy-roosevelt-race -imperialism-national-parks.

15. Christopher Klein, "How Teddy Roosevelt's Belief in a Racial Hierarchy Shaped His Policies," History.com, August 24,

2023, https://www.history.com/news/teddy-roosevelt-race
-imperialism-national-parks.

16. Christopher Klein, "How Teddy Roosevelt's Belief in a
Racial Hierarchy Shaped His Policies," History.com, August 24,
2023, https://www.history.com/news/teddy-roosevelt-race
-imperialism-national-parks.

17. Christopher Klein, "How Teddy Roosevelt's Belief in a
Racial Hierarchy Shaped His Policies," History.com, August 24,
2023, https://www.history.com/news/teddy-roosevelt-race
-imperialism-national-parks.

18. Rachel Chang, "Martin Luther King Jr.'s Famous Speech
Almost Didn't Have the Phrase 'I have a Dream,'" Biography.com,
January 19, 2021, https://www.biography.com/activists/martin
-luther-king-jr-i-have-a-dream-speech.

19. Wikipedia, s.v. "1912 United States presidential election," last modified May 23, 2024, 14:19, https://en.wikipedia
.org/wiki/1912_United_States_presidential_election.

20. Paul Rahe, "Woodrow Wilson: This So-Called
Progressive was a Dedicated Racist," Foundation for Economic
Education, September 17, 2016, https://fee.org/articles/woodrow
-wilson-progressive-and-dedicated-racist/.

21. Becky Little, "How Woodrow Wilson Tried to Reverse Black
American Progress," History.com, September 11, 2023, https://
www.history.com/news/woodrow-wilson-racial-segregation
-jim-crow-ku-klux-klan.

22. Wikipedia, s.v. "The Clansman: A Historical Romance of
the Ku Klux Klan," last modified June 17, 2024, 19:53, https://en
.wikipedia.org/wiki/The_Clansman:_A_Historical_Romance_of
_the_Ku_Klux_Klan.

23. "The Ku Klux Klan, A Secret History," The History Channel, DVD.

24. "The Ku Klux Klan, A Secret History," The History Channel, DVD.

25. Wikipedia, s.v. "Thomas Dixon Jr.," last modified June 23, 2024, 19:25, https://en.wikipedia.org/wiki/Thomas_Dixon_Jr.

26. Fifth Continent, "Joseph Carl Breil 'The Birth of a Nation' 3/3," February 27, 2012, https://www.youtube.com/watch?v=YzBNRecsp4E.

27. Khalbrae, "The Birth of a Nation – Full Movie – (1915) HD – The Masterpiece of Racist Cinema," August 1, 2015, https://www.youtube.com/watch?v=ebtiJH3EOHo&t=50s.

28. "The Theatre Organ Home Page," http://theatreorgans.com/index.html.

29. Wikipedia, s.v. "Theatre organ," last modified May 24, 2024, 19:37, https://en.wikipedia.org/wiki/Theatre_organ.

30. Boardwalk Organs, "Organist Josh Stafford plays Bohemian Rhapsody on the largest pipe organ in the world," October 19, 2020, https://www.youtube.com/watch?v=uHLRgvNh6Lk.

31. Organ Media Foundation, "1928 Wurlitzer Fox Special Organ, Fox Theatre, St. Louis, Missouri, Part 1 of 2," January 18, 2020, https://www.youtube.com/watch?app=desktop&v=kBQdaJr_kMs.

32. TMJ4 News, "World's largest theater organ is being restored in Franklin," March 7, 2022, https://www.youtube.com/watch?v=Issk0AUqnko.

33. History.com Editors, "Woodrow Wilson," History.com, June 6, 2019, https://www.history.com/topics/us-presidents/woodrow-wilson.

34. History.com Editors, "1921 Tulsa Race Massacre," History.com, May 20, 2024, https://www.history.com/topics /roaring-twenties/tulsa-race-massacre.

35. History.com Editors, "Rosewood Massacre," History.com, January 10, 2023, https://www.history.com/topics/early-20th -century-us/rosewood-massacre.

36. Reed Hepler and David White, "The Temperance Movement," Study.com, November 21, 2023, https://study.com /academy/lesson/the-temperance-movement-definition-leaders -timeline.html.

37. "William Gibbs McAdoo," Encyclopedia of World Biography, *Encyclopedia.com*, June 15, 2024, https://www.encyclo pedia.com/history/encyclopedias-almanacs-transcripts-and -maps/william-gibbs-mcadoo.

38. "The Ku Klux Klan, A Secret History," The History Channel, DVD.

39. Adam S. Cohen, "Harvard's Eugenics Era," *Harvard Magazine*, March-April 2016, https://www.harvardmagazine .com/2016/02/harvards-eugenics-era.

40. Adam S. Cohen, "Harvard's Eugenics Era," *Harvard Magazine*, March-April 2016, https://www.harvardmagazine .com/2016/02/harvards-eugenics-era.

41. Wikipedia, s.v. "Frank Hanly," last modified March 2, 2024, 20:37, https://en.wikipedia.org/wiki/Frank_Hanly.

42. Paul Rahe, "Woodrow Wilson: This So-Called Progressive was a Dedicated Racist," Foundation for Economic Education, September 17, 2016, https://fee.org/articles/woodrow -wilson-progressive-and-dedicated-racist/.

43. Adam S. Cohen, "Harvard's Eugenics Era," *Harvard*

Magazine, March–April 2016, https://www.harvardmagazine.com/2016/02/harvards-eugenics-era.

44. Adam S. Cohen, "Harvard's Eugenics Era," *Harvard Magazine*, March–April 2016, https://www.harvardmagazine.com/2016/02/harvards-eugenics-era.

45. Adam S. Cohen, "Harvard's Eugenics Era," *Harvard Magazine*, March–April 2016, https://www.harvardmagazine.com/2016/02/harvards-eugenics-era.

46. Adam S. Cohen, "Harvard's Eugenics Era," *Harvard Magazine*, March–April 2016, https://www.harvardmagazine.com/2016/02/harvards-eugenics-era.

47. Adam S. Cohen, "Harvard's Eugenics Era," *Harvard Magazine*, March–April 2016, https://www.harvardmagazine.com/2016/02/harvards-eugenics-era.

48. Adam S. Cohen, "Harvard's Eugenics Era," *Harvard Magazine*, March–April 2016, https://www.harvardmagazine.com/2016/02/harvards-eugenics-era.

49. Adam S. Cohen, "Harvard's Eugenics Era," *Harvard Magazine*, March–April 2016, https://www.harvardmagazine.com/2016/02/harvards-eugenics-era.

50. Wikipedia, s.v. "Quadroon," last modified June 23, 2024, 01:01, https://en.wikipedia.org/wiki/Quadroon.

51. Wikipedia, s.v. "One-drop rule," last modified May 29, 2024, 18:42, https://en.wikipedia.org/wiki/One-drop_rule.

52. "The 'One Drop Rule' in America, a story," AAREG, https://aaregistry.org/story/the-one-drop-rule-a-brief-story/.

53. Richard Feynman, "Cargo Cult Science," https://www.columbia.edu/cu/neurotheory/Ken/cargo_cult.html.

54. Richard Feynman, "Cargo Cult Science," https://www
.columbia.edu/cu/neurotheory/Ken/cargo_cult.html.

55. The Editors of Encyclopaedia Britannica, "Crispus
Attucks," *Encyclopedia Britannica*, March 1, 2024, https://www
.britannica.com/biography/Crispus-Attucks.

56. "10 Facts: The Continental Army," American Battlefield
Trust, July 7, 2021, https://www.battlefields.org/learn/articles
/10-facts-continental-army.

57. Molly Edmonds and Desiree Bowie, "12 Black Inventors
and Their Innovations That Shaped the World," How Stuff Works,
November 1, 2023, https://science.howstuffworks.com/innovation
/inventions/10-inventions-by-african-americans.htm.

58. Thaddeus Morgan, "8 Black Inventors Who Made Daily
Life Easier," History.com, February 21, 2024, https://www
.history.com/news/8-black-inventors-african-american.

59. Nancy C. Unger, *Fighting Bob Lafollette: The Righteous
Reformer*, (University of North Carolina Press, 2000).

60. Planned Parenthood Mar Monte, "Statement about
Margaret Sanger and PPMM's mission," Planned Parenthood,
April 19, 2021, https://www.plannedparenthood.org/planned
-parenthood-mar-monte/blog/statement-about-margaret-sanger
-and-ppmms-mission.

61. Allison Gordon, "New York's Planned Parenthood will
remove founder's name over her views on eugenics," CNN US,
July 22, 2020, https://www.cnn.com/2020/07/22/us/margaret
-sanger-planned-parenthood-trnd/index.html.

62. Bill Potter, "Margaret Sanger Introduces Her 'Negro
Project', 1939," Landmark Events, June 27, 2017, https://land
markevents.org/history-highlight-week-of-june-25/.

63. Margaret Sanger to Dr C.J. Gamble, letter, December 10, 1939.

64. "The Margaret Sanger Papers Project," New York University, 2001, https://sanger.hosting.nyu.edu/articles/bc_or_race_control/.

65. Kristan Hawkins, "Remove statues of Margaret Sanger, Planned Parenthood founder tied to eugenics and racism," *USA Today*, July 23, 2020, https://www.usatoday.com/story/opinion/2020/07/23/racism-eugenics-margaret-sanger-deserves-no-honors-column/5480192002/.

66. Elvis Presley, "Elvis Presley – In the Ghetto (Official Audio)," December 15, 2013, https://www.youtube.com/watch?v=FJ-robilzhU.

67. Maafa 21, Life Dynamics Incorporated.

68. Maafa 21, Life Dynamics Incorporated.

69. Colman McCarthy, "Jackson's Reversal on Abortion," *The Washington Post*, May 20, 1988, https://www.washingtonpost.com/archive/opinions/1988/05/21/jacksons-reversal-on-abortion/dd9e1637-020d-447b-9329-95ec67e41fd5/.

70. Larry Aldelman "Race the power of an illusion Documentary," California Newsreel.

71. Larry Aldelman "Race the power of an illusion Documentary," California Newsreel.

72. Larry Aldelman "Race the power of an illusion Documentary," California Newsreel.

73. Antero Pietila, *Not In My Neighborhood, How Bigotry Shaped A Great American City*, (Chicago: Ivan R Dee, 2010).

74. Antero Pietila, *Not In My Neighborhood, How Bigotry Shaped A Great American City*, (Chicago: Ivan R Dee, 2010).

75. Ronald Reagan Quotes, BrainyQuote, https://www.brainyquote.com/authors/ronald-reagan-quotes.

76. Ronald Reagan Quotes, BrainyQuote, https://www.brainyquote.com/authors/ronald-reagan-quotes.

77. Ronald Reagan Quotes, BrainyQuote, https://www.brainyquote.com/authors/ronald-reagan-quotes.

78. Ronald Reagan Quotes, BrainyQuote, https://www.brainyquote.com/authors/ronald-reagan-quotes.

79. Ronald Reagan Quotes, BrainyQuote, https://www.brainyquote.com/authors/ronald-reagan-quotes.

80. The Fairmont Group, "Thomas Sowell Speaking at The Fairmont Conference 1980," May 9, 2018, https://www.youtube.com/watch?v=c6rEq-p6J0Y.

81. Hoover Institution, "Glenn Loury, Ian Rowe, and Robert Woodson Debunk Myths about the Black Experience in America," July 25, 2022, https://www.youtube.com/watch?v=hIiyIEyUxu8.

82. Wikipedia, s.v. "David Simon," last modified June 21, 2024, 20:18, https://en.wikipedia.org/wiki/David_Simon.

83. LibertyPen, "Thomas Sowell - Legacy of the Welfare State," July 27, 2015, https://www.youtube.com/watch?v=lm-FqtAOSB8.

84. Thomas Sowell, *Wealth, Poverty and Politics*, (New York: Basic Books, 2015).

85. "Election of 1860," National Park Service, https://www.nps.gov/subjects/inauguration/election-of-1860.htm.

CHAPTER 5: CRIMINAL JUSTICE REFORM

1. Wikipedia, s.v. "Comprehensive Crime Control Act of 1984," last modified January 24, 2024, 03:38, https://en.wikipedia.org/wiki/Comprehensive_Crime_Control_Act_of_1984.

2. "1994 Bill Clinton – Three Strikes and You are Out," State of the Union History, http://www.stateoftheunionhistory .com/2019/01/1994-bill-clinton-three-strikes-and-you.html.

3. America Rising PAC, "Joe Biden Warns Of 'Predators On Our Streets' Who Were 'Beyond The Pale' In 1993 Crime Speech," June 18, 2019, https://www.youtube.com/watch?v=7oDHSt-CKtc.

4. Roll Call 416 H.R. 3355, 103rd Cong., (1994).

5. Rool Call H.R. 3355, 103rd Cong., (1994).

6. *Violent Crime Control and Law Enforcement Act of 1994*, H.R. 3355, 103rd Cong. (1994).

7. The Rubin Report, "Watch Bill Maher's Face as Dem Guest Attacks White Liberal's Insane Ideas | DM CLIPS | Rubin Report," Rumble.com, February 14, 2023, https://rumble.com/v29jva8 -watch-bill-mahers-face-as-dem-guest-attacks-white-liberals -insane-ideas-dm-.html.

8. Real Time with Bill Maher, "Overtime: Malcolm Nance, Kristen Soltis Anderson | Real Time with Bill Maher (HBO)," February 11, 2023, https://www.youtube.com/watch? v=TL0DzsV8rhc.

9. *The New York Times*, "Second Presidential Debate | Election 2016 | The New York Times," October 9, 2016, https://www .youtube.com/watch?v=rfq0Yw2sMq0.

10. Ralph H. de Similien, M.D., M.S., M.Ed. and Adamma Okorafor, M.D, "Suicide by Cop: A Psychiatric Phenomenon," *The American Journal of Psychiatry*, 12, no. 1, January 2017, https://doi .org/10.1176/appi.ajp-rj.2017.120107.

11. Thomas sowell Quotes, AZ Quotes, https://www.azquotes .com/author/13901-Thomas_Sowell.

12. C-Span, "C-SPAN: President Reagan 1981 Inaugural

Address," January 14, 2009, https://www.youtube.com/watch?v=hpPt7xGx4Xo.

13. Doug Koenigsberg, *Discovering City Ministry Secrets of engaging a city and its people*, (Baltimore: Uptown Press, 2018).

14. Kaitlyn Schallhorn, "What is the First Step Act? 5 things to know about the criminal justice reform law," *Fox News*, December 19, 2018, https://www.foxnews.com/politics/what-is-first-step-act-5-things-to-know-about-the-criminal-justice-reform-law.

15. Ramishah Maruf, Parija Kavilanz and Cheri Mossburg, "Target says it will close nine stores in major cities across four states because of theft and organized crime," *CNN Business*, September 27, 2023, https://edition.cnn.com/2023/09/26/business/target-retail-theft-store-closures/index.html.

16. Ramishah Maruf, Parija Kavilanz and Cheri Mossburg, "Target says it will close nine stores in major cities across four states because of theft and organized crime," *CNN Business*, September 27, 2023, https://edition.cnn.com/2023/09/26/business/target-retail-theft-store-closures/index.html.

17. Steve Byas, "National Anthem Protests," *NewAmerican*, 32, no. 20, October 2016, https://thenewamerican.com/print/national-anthem-protests/.

CHAPTER 6: NATIONAL ANTHEM

1. Steve Byas, "National Anthem Protests," *NewAmerican*, 32, no. 20, October 2016, https://thenewamerican.com/print/national-anthem-protests/.

2. Jefferson Morley, "It is time to examine the words and the origins of our national anthem, another neo-Confederate symbol,"

salon, August 27, 2017, https://www.salon.com/2017/08/27/it-is
-time-to-examine-the-words-and-the-origins-of-our-national
-anthem-another-neo-confederate-symbol_partner/.

3. Jefferson Morley, "It is time to examine the words and the
origins of our national anthem, another neo-Confederate symbol," *salon*, August 27, 2017, https://www.salon.com/2017/08/27
/it-is-time-to-examine-the-words-and-the-origins-of-our
-national-anthem-another-neo-confederate-symbol_partner/.

4. Wikipedia, s.v. "James Weldon Johnson," last modified
June 8, 2024, 20:43, https://en.wikipedia.org/wiki/James_Weldon
_Johnson.

5. Wikipedia, s.v. "James Weldon Johnson," last modified
June 8, 2024, 20:43, https://en.wikipedia.org/wiki/James_Weldon
_Johnson.

6. Wikipedia, s.v. "James Weldon Johnson," last modified
June 8, 2024, 20:43, https://en.wikipedia.org/wiki/James_Weldon
_Johnson.

7. The Editors of Encyclopaedia Britannica, "James Weldon
Johnson," *Encyclopedia Britannica*, June 22, 2024, https://www
.britannica.com/biography/James-Weldon-Johnson.

8. "James Weldon Johnson," NAACP, https://naacp.org
/find-resources/history-explained/civil-rights-leaders/james
-weldon-johnson.

9. "James Weldon Johnson," NAACP, https://naacp.org
/find-resources/history-explained/civil-rights-leaders/james
-weldon-johnson.

10. *The American Heritage Dictionary of the English Language*,
1981 ed., s.v. "liberal."

11. Cate Lineberry, "The Story Behind the Star Spangled

NOTES

Banner," *Smithsonian Magazine*, March 1, 2007, https://www.smith
sonianmag.com/history/the-story-behind-the-star-spangled
-banner-149220970/.

12. "Joseph Biden Sr., 86, the father of..." *The Baltimore Sun*,
September 3, 2002, https://www.baltimoresun.com/2002/09/03
/joseph-biden-sr-86-the-father-of/.

13. "Joseph Biden Sr., 86, the father of..." *The Baltimore Sun*,
September 3, 2002, https://www.baltimoresun.com/2002/09/03
/joseph-biden-sr-86-the-father-of/.

14. Wikipedia, s.v. "J. Charles Linthicum," last modified
February 28, 2024, 02:02, https://en.wikipedia.org/wiki/J._Charles
_Linthicum.

15. History.com Editors, "The Star-Spangled Banner,"
History.com, June 13, 2024, https://www.history.com/topics/19th
-century/the-star-spangled-banner.

16. History.com Editors, "The Star-Spangled Banner," History.
com, June 13, 2024, https://www.history.com/topics/19th-century
/the-star-spangled-banner.

17. Tom Ozimek, "Black National Anthem at Super Bowl
Stirs Controversy," *The Epoch Times*, February 13, 2023, https://
www.theepochtimes.com/sports/black-national-anthem-at
-super-bowl-stirs-controversy-5053931.

18. Jams Weldon Johnson, "Lieft Every Voice and Sing," Poetry
Foundation, https://www.poetryfoundation.org/poems/46549
/lift-every-voice-and-sing.

19. "Rewriting History: The Lee-Jackson Monument in
Baltimore," Lee Jackson Monument, https://leejacksonmonument
.weebly.com/.

20. "Rewriting History: The Lee-Jackson Monument in

Baltimore," Lee Jackson Monument, https://leejacksonmonument.weebly.com/.

21. "Rewriting History: The Lee-Jackson Monument in Baltimore," Lee Jackson Monument, https://leejacksonmonument.weebly.com/.

CHAPTER 7: PROPAGANDA FOR THE NEW AGE

1. Wikipedia, s.v. "Ivan Pavlov," last modified June 12, 2024, 15:22, https://en.wikipedia.org/wiki/Ivan_Pavlov.

2. The Post Millenial Live, "Jimmy Dore: "This is the world we're living in, the stuff that we were supposed to be afraid of Donald Trump doing, Joe Biden is doing and the corporate media gets America to cheer it on..." Rumble, February 16, 2023, https://rumble.com/v29s5ws-february-16-2023.html.

3. Rachel Chang, "Martin Luther King Jr.'s Famous Speech Almost Didn't Have the Phrase 'I have a Dream,'" Biography.com, January 19, 2021, https://www.biography.com/activists/martin-luther-king-jr-i-have-a-dream-speech.

4. The Post Millenial Live, "Jimmy Dore: "This is the world we're living in, the stuff that we were supposed to be afraid of Donald Trump doing, Joe Biden is doing and the corporate media gets America to cheer it on..." Rumble, February 16, 2023, https://rumble.com/v29s5ws-february-16-2023.html.

5. The Hill, "INSIDE TWITTER FILES: Authors Reveal How Emails EXPOSE HUGE Censorship Campaign On Platform," March 11, 2023, https://www.youtube.com/watch?v=t1m96yeSjbo.

6. Branko Marcetic, "Why the Twitter Files Are in Fact a Big Deal," Jacobin, December 29, 2022, https://jacobin

.com/2022/12/twitter-files-censorship-content-moderation-intelligence-agencies-surveillance.

7. Paul Bedard, "Regrets, you've had a few: 20% want Biden vote back," *Washington Examiner*, September 3, 2021, https://www.washingtonexaminer.com/news/washington-secrets/634065/regrets-youve-had-a-few-20-want-biden-vote-back/.

8. The Post Millennial, "FLASHBACK: 16% of Biden voters would have voted differently if Hunter Biden laptop story was not suppressed by media, big tech," *Post Millennial*, March 17, 2022, https://thepostmillennial.com/flashback-16-of-biden-voters.

9. Johnathan Jones, "Poll: 17% of Biden Voters Would Have Abandoned Him if They Knew About Stories the Media Censored," *The Western Journal*, November 24, 2020, https://www.westernjournal.com/poll-17-biden-voters-abandoned-knew-stories-media-censored/.

CHAPTER 8: SOCIALISM IN OUR MIDST

1. Wikipedia, s.v. "Whittaker Chambers," last modified May 30, 2024, 20:00, https://en.wikipedia.org/wiki/Whittaker_Chambers.

2. Nicholas von Hoffman, "WAS MCCARTHY RIGHT ABOUT THE LEFT?" *The Washington Post*, April 14, 1996, https://www.washingtonpost.com/archive/opinions/1996/04/14/was-mccarthy-right-about-the-left/a0dc6726-e2fd-4a31-bcdd-5f352acbf5de/.

3. Eduardo Corrochio, "Yuri Bezmenov (Full Interview) with G. Edward Griffin," September 5, 2020, https://www.youtube.com/watch?v=s2b-IoYqisc.

4. Samuel Sheetz, ""We Win; They Lose": The Staggering Simplicity of Reagan's Grand Strategy," *The Daily Signal*, December 10, 2011, https://www.dailysignal.com/2011/12/10/we-win-they-lose-the-staggering-simplicity-of-reagan%E2%80%99s-grand-strategy/.

5. Samuel Sheetz, ""We Win; They Lose": The Staggering Simplicity of Reagan's Grand Strategy," *The Daily Signal*, December 10, 2011, https://www.dailysignal.com/2011/12/10/we-win-they-lose-the-staggering-simplicity-of-reagan%E2%80%99s-grand-strategy/.

6. Kaylee McGhee White, "Colleges are turning young people socialist in a few ways," *The Washington Examiner*, October 30, 2019, https://www.washingtonexaminer.com/opinion/1927408/colleges-are-turning-young-people-socialist-in-a-few-ways/.

7. John Miltimore and Dan Sanchez, "The New York Times Reported 'the Mainstreaming of Marxism in US Colleges' 30 Years Ago. Today, We See the Results," Foundation for Economic Education, September 10, 2020, https://fee.org/articles/the-new-york-times-reported-the-mainstreaming-of-marxism-in-us-colleges-30-years-ago-today-we-see-the-results/.

8. Dana Hanson, "The 10 Richest People in Venezuela," Money Inc, April 11, 2023, https://moneyinc.com/richest-people-in-venezuela/.

9. Dana Hanson, "The 10 Richest People in Venezuela," Money Inc, April 11, 2023, https://moneyinc.com/richest-people-in-venezuela/.

10. Wikipedia, s.v. "Hugo Chávez," last modified May 2, 2024, 15:09, https://en.wikipedia.org/wiki/Hugo_Ch%C3%A1vez.

11. The Editors of Encyclopaedia Britannica, "Pol Pot," *Encyclopedia Britannica*, May 15, 2024, https://www.britannica.com/biography/Pol-Pot.

12. "The 15 Worst Atrocities Committed By Fidel Castro," TheRichest, https://www.therichest.com/shocking/the-15-worst-atrocities-committed-by-fidel-castro/.

13. Valerie Strauss and Daniel Southerland, "How Many Died? New Evidence Suggests Far Higher Numbers for the Victims of Mao Zedong's Era," *The Washington Post*, July 19, 1994, https://www.washingtonpost.com/archive/politics/1994/07/17/how-many-died-new-evidence-suggests-far-higher-numbers-for-the-victims-of-mao-zedongs-era/01044df5-03dd-49f4-a453-a033c5287bce/.

14. Will, "10 World Dictators Who Killed The Most People," Eskify, http://eskify.com/10-world-dictators-who-killed-the-most-people/.

15. history1917, "Stalin's Policy of Collectivisation and the Soviet Famines: A Historical Overview," Explaining History Podcast, March 28, 2023, https://explaininghistory.org/2023/03/28/stalins-policy-of-collectivisation-and-the-soviet-famines-a-historical-overview/.

16. history1917, "Stalin's Policy of Collectivisation and the Soviet Famines: A Historical Overview," Explaining History Podcast, March 28, 2023, https://explaininghistory.org/2023/03/28/stalins-policy-of-collectivisation-and-the-soviet-famines-a-historical-overview/.

17. history1917, "Stalin's Policy of Collectivisation and the Soviet Famines: A Historical Overview," Explaining History Podcast, March 28, 2023, https://explaininghistory.org/2023

/03/28/stalins-policy-of-collectivisation-and-the-soviet-famines
-a-historical-overview/.

18. Patrick J. Kiger, "How Joseph Stalin Starved Millions in the Ukrainian Famine," History.com, April 16, 2019, https://www .history.com/news/ukrainian-famine-stalin.

19. "Communism," National Geographic, https://education .nationalgeographic.org/resource/communism/.

20. Austin Cline, "Karl Marx on Religion as the Opium of the People," Learn Religions, January 5, 2019, https://www.learn religions.com/karl-marx-on-religion-251019.

21. Chip Berlet, "Mussolini on the Corporate State," Political Research Associates, January 12, 2005, https://politicalresearch .org/2005/01/12/mussolini-corporate-state.

22. Robert Soucy, "fascism," *Encyclopedia Britannica*, May 27, 2024, https://www.britannica.com/topic/fascism.

23. Robert Soucy, "fascism," *Encyclopedia Britannica*, May 27, 2024, https://www.britannica.com/topic/fascism.

24. History.com Editors, "Molotov-Ribbentrop Pact," History.com, November 15, 2022, https://www.history.com /topics/world-war-ii/molotov-ribbentrop-pact.

25. Jesse Greenspan, "When Stalin Was Caught Napping," History.com, March 11, 2019, https://www.history.com/news /how-stalin-was-caught-napping.

26. History.com Editors, "Molotov-Ribbentrop Pact," History.com, November 15, 2022, https://www.history.com /topics/world-war-ii/molotov-ribbentrop-pact.

27. Kath.Net, "'If fascism ever comes to America, it will come in the name of liberalism' (Ronald Reagan," January 10 2021, https://www.youtube.com/watch?v=QwFvaSZfXNk.

28. "Lyndon B. Johnson Quotes – Page 11," AZ Quotes, https://www.azquotes.com/author/7511-Lyndon_B_Johnson?p=11.

29. U.S. Department of Labor, http://www.dol.gov/dol/aboutdol/history/moynchapter2.htm.

30. U.S. Department of Labor, http://www.dol.gov/dol/aboutdol/history/moynchapter2.htm.

31. Kath.Net, "'If fascism ever comes to America, it will come in the name of liberalism' (Ronald Reagan," January 10 2021, https://www.youtube.com/watch?v=QwFvaSZfXNk.

32. Karen Grigsby Bates, "Moynihan Black Poverty Report Revisited 50 Years Later," *NPR*, June 13, 2013, https://www.npr.org/sections/codeswitch/2013/06/13/190982608/moynihan-black-poverty-report-revisited-fifty-years-later.

33. Wikipedia, s.v. "Daniel Patrick Moynihan," last modified April 26, 2024, 15:58, https://en.wikipedia.org/wiki/Daniel_Patrick_Moynihan/.

34. Thomas Sowell TV, "How the Welfare state ruined black families," October 14, 2022, https://www.youtube.com/watch?app=desktop&v=RIwkZYdSelE.

35. LibertyPen, "Thomas Sowell - Poverty & Dependence," February 13, 2012, https://www.youtube.com/watch?v=ZlsHNzp5SoM.

36. LibertyPen, "Thomas Sowell - Poverty & Dependence," February 13, 2012, https://www.youtube.com/watch?v=ZlsHNzp5SoM.

37. LibertyPen, "Thomas Sowell - Poverty & Dependence," February 13, 2012, https://www.youtube.com/watch?v=ZlsHNzp5SoM.

38. The Editors of Encyclopaedia Britannica, "Frankfurt

School," *Encyclopedia Britannica*, April 12, 2024, https://www
.britannica.com/topic/Frankfurt-School.

39. The Editors of Encyclopaedia Britannica, "Frankfurt
School," *Encyclopedia Britannica*, April 12, 2024, https://www
.britannica.com/topic/Frankfurt-School.

40. The Editors of Encyclopaedia Britannica, "Frankfurt
School," *Encyclopedia Britannica*, April 12, 2024, https://www
.britannica.com/topic/Frankfurt-School.

41. The Editors of Encyclopaedia Britannica, "Frankfurt
School," *Encyclopedia Britannica*, April 12, 2024, https://www
.britannica.com/topic/Frankfurt-School.

CHAPTER 9: CHRISTIAN NATIONALISM, OH MY!

1. Best Movies By Farr, "Lions and Tigers and Bears, Oh My!
- "The Wizard of Oz" (1939)," October 27, 2016, https://www
.youtube.com/watch?v=-HrfbV16-FQ.

2. Neil J. Young, "The Mundane History of White Christian
Nationalism," Religion & Politics, February 14, 2023, https://
religionandpolitics.org/2023/02/14/the-mundane-history-of
-white-christian-nationalism/.

3. Ja'han Jones, "Troubling data shows many Americans
are pining to become a theocracy," MSNBC, February 13, 2023,
https://www.msnbc.com/the-reidout/reidout-blog/christian
-nationalism-report-prri-rcna70193.

4. Andrew Whitehead, "The Growing Anti-Democratic Threat
of Christian Nationalism in the U.S.," *Time*, May 27, 2021, https://
time.com/6052051/anti-democratic-threat-christian-nationalism/.

5. John Burnett, "Christian nationalism is still thriving —
and is a force for returning Trump to power," *NPR*, January

23, 2022, https://www.npr.org/2022/01/14/1073215412/christian
-nationalism-donald-trump.

6. Guthrie Graves-Fitzsimmons and Maggie Siddiai, "Christian Nationalism Is 'Single Biggest Threat' to America's Religious Freedom," Cap20, April 13, 2022, https://www.americanprogress.org/article/christian-nationalism-is-single-biggest-threat-to-americas-religious-freedom/.

7. Conn Carroll, "The Left's new Christian nationalism scare," *The Washington Examiner*, February 15, 2023, https://www.washingtonexaminer.com/opinion/1895201/the-lefts-new-christian-nationalism-scare/.

8. The Editors of Encyclopaedia Britannica, "Great Awakening," *Encyclopedia Britannica*, March 25, 2024, https://www.britannica.com/event/Great-Awakening.

9. History.com Editors, "Great Awakening," History.com, September 20, 2019, https://www.history.com/topics/european-history/great-awakening.

10. History.com Editors, "John Brown," History.com, June 27, 2023, https://www.history.com/topics/slavery/john-brown.

11. The Editors of Holocaust Enecylopedia, "Dietrich Bonhoeffer," *Holocaust Encyclopedia*, https://encyclopedia.ushmm.org/content/en/article/dietrich-bonhoeffer.

12. "Sophie Scholl and the White Rose," The National WWII Museum, February 22, 2020, https://www.nationalww2museum.org/war/articles/sophie-scholl-and-white-rose.

13. Michael Ray, "White Rose," *Encyclopedia Britannica*, April 23, 2024, https://www.britannica.com/topic/White-Rose.

14. Michael Ray, "White Rose," *Encyclopedia Britannica*, April 23, 2024, https://www.britannica.com/topic/White-Rose.

15. Michael Ray, "White Rose," *Encyclopedia Britannica*, April 23, 2024, https://www.britannica.com/topic/White-Rose.

16. Michael Ray, "White Rose," *Encyclopedia Britannica*, April 23, 2024, https://www.britannica.com/topic/White-Rose.

17. F. William Engdahl, "Is Gene Editing the New Name for Eugenics? 'Enter Bill Gates,'" Global Research, March 7, 2024, https://www.globalresearch.ca/is-gene-editing-the-new-name-for-eugenics/5645101.

18. Philip K. Wilson, "eugenics," *Encyclopedia Britannica*, June 19, 2024, https://www.britannica.com/science/eugenics-genetics.

CHAPTER 10: IMMIGRATION REFORM

1. "Did Reagan Support 'Amnesty' for Illegal Immigrants?" Wild World of History, https://www.wildworldofhistory.com/blog/did-reagan-support-amnesty-for-illegal-immigrants.

2. NPR Staff, "A Reagan Legacy: Amnesty for Illegal Immigrants," *NPR*, July 4, 2010, https://www.npr.org/2010/07/04/128303672/a-reagan-legacy-amnesty-for-illegal-immigrants.

3. NPR Staff, "A Reagan Legacy: Amnesty for Illegal Immigrants," *NPR*, July 4, 2010, https://www.npr.org/2010/07/04/128303672/a-reagan-legacy-amnesty-for-illegal-immigrants.

4. NPR Staff, "A Reagan Legacy: Amnesty for Illegal Immigrants," *NPR*, July 4, 2010, https://www.npr.org/2010/07/04/128303672/a-reagan-legacy-amnesty-for-illegal-immigrants.

5. Bill George, "1984 - Ronald Reagan on Amnesty," January 21, 2010, https://www.youtube.com/watch?v=WxL3OU1dwmI.

6. PBS NewsHour, "Reagan vs. Mondale: The second 1984 presidential debate," September 26, 2020, https://www.youtube.com/watch?v=5SbsCaRYW6w&t=3208s.

7. "Barbara Jordan and the U.S. Commission on Immigration Reform," The CAIRO Report, https://www.cairco.org/reference /barbara-jordan-us-commission-immigration-reform.

8. "Barbara Jordan and the U.S. Commission on Immigration Reform," The CAIRO Report, https://www.cairco.org/reference /barbara-jordan-us-commission-immigration-reform.

9. "Barbara Jordan and the U.S. Commission on Immigration Reform," The CAIRO Report, https://www.cairco.org/reference /barbara-jordan-us-commission-immigration-reform.

10. "Barbara Jordan and the U.S. Commission on Immigration Reform," The CAIRO Report, https://www.cairco.org/reference /barbara-jordan-us-commission-immigration-reform.

11. NumbersUSA, "Barbara Jordan's Vision of Immigration Reform," https://www.numbersusa.com/resource-article/barbara -jordans-vision-immigration-reform.

12. NumbersUSA, "Barbara Jordan's Vision of Immigration Reform," https://www.numbersusa.com/resource-article/barbara -jordans-vision-immigration-reform.

13. NumbersUSA, "Barbara Jordan's Vision of Immigration Reform," https://www.numbersusa.com/resource-article/barbara -jordans-vision-immigration-reform.

14. NumbersUSA, "Barbara Jordan's Vision of Immigration Reform," https://www.numbersusa.com/resource-article/barbara -jordans-vision-immigration-reform.

15. Rusy Weiss, "Whoops: Congressman Accidentally Reveals Why Democrats Really Want Amnesty," *The Political Insider*, February 16, 2015, https://thepoliticalinsider.com/whoops -congressman-accidentally-reveals-democrats-really-want -amnesty/.

16. Digitas Daily, "Rep. Luis Gutiérrez brags amnesty could bring 4-5 million new Democrats," July 25, 2014, https://www.youtube.com/watch?v=-cTFzUezEyo.

17. PolitiFact Staff, "Fact-checking Donald Trump's 2020 State of the Union address," PolitiFact, February 5, 2020, https://www.politifact.com/article/2020/feb/05/fact-checking-2020-state-union-address/.

18. CNN Staff, "Fact-checking the 2020 State of the Union," *CNN Politics*, February 6, 2020, https://www.cnn.com/2020/02/04/politics/fact-check-trump-state-of-the-union-2020/index.html.

19. *CNN*, "Trump's entire 2020 State of the Union address," February 5, 2020, https://www.youtube.com/watch?v=zNECVmfJtxc.

20. Alex J. Rouhandeh, "Drug Cartels Steer the Flow of Migrants at Border; Can Biden Make Mexico Stop Them?" *Newsweek*, December 3, 2021, https://www.newsweek.com/drug-cartels-steer-flow-migrants-border-can-biden-make-mexico-stop-them-1655643.

21. E.D. Cauchi, "Mexican drug cartels pay Americans to smuggle weapons across the border, intelligence documents show," *CBS News*, September 18, 2023, https://www.cbsnews.com/news/mexican-drug-cartels-american-weapons-smuggled-across-border/.

22. Miriam Jordan, "Smuggling Migrants at the Border Now a Billion-Dollar Business," *The New York Times*, July 25, 2022, https://www.nytimes.com/2022/07/25/us/migrant-smuggling-evolution.html.

23. "What is Fentanyl?" National Institute on Drug Abuse, May 12, 2022, https://nida.nih.gov/research-topics/trends-statistics/infographics/what-fentanyl.

CHAPTER 11: THE BIG SWITCH—YES, BUT WHY?

1. Becky Little, "How the 'Party of Lincoln' Won Over the Once Democratic South," History.com, April 10, 2019, https://www.history.com/news/how-the-party-of-lincoln-won-over-the-once-democratic-south.

2. "Confederate Memorial," Arlington National Cemetery, https://www.arlingtoncemetery.mil/Explore/Monuments-and-Memorials/Confederate-Memorial.

3. Rick Chromey, "The Big Switch That Wasn't: The Dixiecrats, Race and 1964," Dr. Rick Chromey, May 24, 2023, https://rickchromey.com/the-big-switch-that-wasnt-the-dixiecrats-race-and-1964/.

4. Hr. 7152. Passage., govtrack.us, June 19, 1964, https://www.govtrack.us/congress/votes/88-1964/s409.

5. Tony Basley, "Vince Lombardi - What the hell's going on out here!?" September 13, 2012, https://www.youtube.com/watch?v=vyRSV9eqTUY.

6. Wikipedia, s.v. "James Eastland," last modified June 25, 2024, 23:54, https://en.wikipedia.org/wiki/James_Eastland.

7. https://en.wikipedia.org/wiki/George_Wallace

8. https://www.npr.org/2013/01/14/169080969/segregation-forever-a-fiery-pledge-forgiven-but-not-forgotten

CHAPTER 12: THE COACH

1. Tony Basley, "Vince Lombardi - What the hell's going on out here!?" September 13, 2012, https://www.youtube.com/watch?v=vyRSV9eqTUY.

2. Chris McGreal, "Rachel Dolezal: 'I wasn't identifying as black to upset people. I was being me,'" *The Guardian*,

December 13, 2015, https://www.theguardian.com/us-news/2015 /dec/13/rachel-dolezal-i-wasnt-identifying-as-black-to-upset -people-i-was-being-me.

3. Michael Brendan Dougherty, "Elizabeth Warren's Native American Problem Isn't Going Away," *National Review*, September 30, 2019, https://www.nationalreview.com/2019 /09/elizabeth-warren-native-american-controversy-not-going -away/.

4. Dion J. Pierre, "Separate but Equal, Again," National Association of Scholars, April 24, 2019, https://www.nas.org /reports/separate-but-equal-again/full-report.

5. Post Editorial Board, "31 Harvard student groups' despicable letter backing Hamas exposes the deep sickness of US academia," *New York Post*, October 9, 2023, https://nypost .com/2023/10/09/despicable-harvard-31-support-hamas-attack -and-kidnappings/.

6. Khaleda Rahman, "Harvard Students Blaming Israel for Hamas Attacks Sparks Fury: 'Despicable,'" *Newsweek*, October 9, 2023, https://www.newsweek.com/harvard-students -blaming-israel-hamas-attacks-fury-1832997.

7. Joseph Ax and Gabriella Borter, "US colleges become flash-points for protests over Israel-Hamas war," Reuters, October 14, 2023, https://www.reuters.com/world/us/us-colleges-become -flashpoints-protests-both-sides-israel-hamas-war-2023-10-13/.

8. Scott Neuman, "What did Hamas aim to gain by its brazen attack on Israel? Here's what to know," *NPR*, October 12, 2023, https://www.npr.org/2023/10/12/1204881032/hamas-israel -attack-palestinians.

9. "Current US Inflation Rates: 2000-2024," US Inflation

Calculator, https://www.usinflationcalculator.com/inflation/current-inflation-rates/.

10. "The Border Report: Nearly 1.6 million 'gotaways' in U.S. since January 2021," *The Washington Examiner*, August 28, 2023, https://www.washingtonexaminer.com/policy/immigration/2580643/the-border-report-nearly-1-6-million-gotaways-in-u-s-since-january-2021/.

11. Terri Moon Cronk, "Biden Announces Full U.S. Troop Withdrawal From Afghanistan by Sept. 11," U.S. Department of Defense, April 14, 2021, https://www.defense.gov/News/News-Stories/Article/Article/2573268/biden-announces-full-us-troop-withdrawal-from-afghanistan-by-sept-11/.

12. Tom Rogan, "British Parliament rages against Biden," *The Washington Examiner*, August 19, 2021, https://www.washington-examiner.com/opinion/455097/british-parliament-rages-against-biden/.

13. "Constitution of the United States," Constitution Annotated, https://constitution.congress.gov/constitution/preamble/.

14. Adam S. Cohen, "Harvard's Eugenics Era," *Harvard Magazine*, March–April 2016, https://www.harvardmagazine.com/2016/02/harvards-eugenics-era.

15. "A Brief History of the Boston Brahmin," New England Historical Society, https://newenglandhistoricalsociety.com/brief-history-boston-brahmin/.

16. Wikipedia, s.v. "Obadiah Bush," last modified June 27, 2024, 11:42, https://en.wikipedia.org/wiki/Obadiah_Bush.

17. Wikipedia, s.v. "Marvin Pierce," last modified April 28, 2024, 08:32, https://en.wikipedia.org/wiki/Marvin_Pierce.

18. Gabe Ferris, "Biden signs CHIPS Act, intended to relieve the

pandemic-era computer chip shortage," *ABC News*, August 9, 2022, https://abcnews.go.com/Politics/biden-signs-chips-act-intended -relieve-pandemic-era/story?id=88143303.

19. Mary Bellis, "Who Invented the Microchip?" ThoughtCo., May 24, 2024, https://www.thoughtco.com/what-is-a-microchip -1991410.

20. "A Brief History of the Boston Brahmin," New England Historical Society, https://newenglandhistoricalsociety.com /brief-history-boston-brahmin/.

21. Peter Schweizer, *Red Handed*, (New York: HarperCollins, 2022).

22. Wells King, "Globalization: America's Biggest Bipartisan Mistake | Opinion," Newsweek, March 31, 2022, https://www .newsweek.com/globalization-americas-biggest-bipartisan -mistake-opinion-1693377.

23. Blackpast, "(2004) Bill Cosby, 'The Pound Cake Speech,'" BlackPast, January 28, 2007, https://www.blackpast .org/african-american-history/2004-bill-cosby-pound-cake- speech/.

24. Mrs. Berry, "Bill Cosby's Infamous 'Pound Cake' Speech," September 28, 2018, https://www.youtube.com/watch? v=U_IGlwgVGoo.

25. Barbara Mikkelson, "Bill Cosby on Blaming White People," Snopes, October 15, 2005, https://www.snopes.com/fact -check/cos-cause/.

26. *CNN*, "One video to explain Jon Gruber and Obamacare," November 18, 2014, https://www.youtube.com/watch?v=tLOV4o UXawg.

27. Wikipedia, v.s. "Andrea Constand v. Bill Cosby," last

modified June 26, 2024, 22:10, https://en.wikipedia.org/wiki/Andrea_Constand_v._Bill_Cosby.

28. *CNN*, "One video to explain Jon Gruber and Obamacare," November 18, 2014, https://www.youtube.com/watch?v=tLOV4oUXawg.

29. *CNN*, "'Stupidity' remark haunts Obamacare consultant," November 13, 2014, https://www.youtube.com/watch?v=g6wljfbRaDM.

30. Avik Roy, "ACA Architect: 'The Stupidity Of The American Voter' Led Us To Hide Obamacare's True Costs From The Public," *Forbes*, December 18, 2014, https://www.forbes.com/sites/theapothecary/2014/11/10/aca-architect-the-stupidity-of-the-american-voter-led-us-to-hide-obamacares-tax-hikes-and-subsidies-from-the-public/?sh=25ef65957c05.

31. *Fox News*, "Tucker takes on ObamaCare architect Jonathan Gruber," January 25, 2017, https://www.youtube.com/watch?v=kvDlBIaZV9w.

32. Dr. Peter A. McCullough, MD and John Leake, "Dietrich Bonhoeffer's Theory: 'On Stupidity,'" *Epoch Times*, February 27, 2023, https://www.theepochtimes.com/health/dietrich-bonhoeffers-theory-on-stupidity-5084426.

33. Sprouts, "Bonhoeffer's Theory of Stupidity," October 15, 2021, https://www.youtube.com/watch?v=ww47bR86wSc.

34. US Debt Clock, https://www.usdebtclock.org/.

35. Niall McCarthy, "More Than 220,000 Bridges Need Repair Work In The U.S. [Infographic]," *Forbes*, April 6, 2021, https://www.forbes.com/sites/niallmccarthy/2021/04/06/more-than-220000-bridges-need-repair-work-in-the-us-infographic/?sh=19e9ad7632e2.

36. Nick Gillespie, "Obama's War on Journalism: 'An Unconstitutional Act,'" *Daily Beast*, May 22, 2013, https://www.thedailybeast.com/obamas-war-on-journalism-an-unconstitutional-act.

37. Jill Colvin, "DNC, Clinton campaign agree to Steele dossier funding fine," *Associated Press*, March 31, 2022, https://apnews.com/article/russia-ukraine-2022-midterm-elections-business-elections-presidential-elections-5468774d18e8c46f81b55e926 0b13e93.

38. Bruce Golding, "79% say 'truthful' coverage of Hunter Biden's laptop would have changed 2020 election," *New York Post*, August 26, 2022, https://nypost.com/2022/08/26/2020-election-outcome-would-differ-with-hunter-biden-laptop-coverage-poll/.

39. Jerry Dunleavy, "Intelligence leaders asked to sign Hunter Biden laptop letter speak out: 'Declined to sign,'" *The Washington Examiner*, May 15, 2023, https://www.washingtonexaminer.com/news/564480/intelligence-leaders-asked-to-sign-hunter-biden-laptop-letter-speak-out-declined-to-sign/.

40. Nick Gillespie, "Obama's War on Journalism: 'An Unconstitutional Act,'" *Daily Beast*, May 22, 2013, https://www.thedailybeast.com/obamas-war-on-journalism-an-unconstitutional-act.

41. NFL Films, "Vince Lombardi: The Coach Who Put Green Bay on the Map | A Football Life," February 4, 2021, https://www.youtube.com/watch?v=njlGLMYopLo&t=2317s.

42. Evan "Tex" Western, "Vince Lombardi Allowed 'Nothing But Acceptance' In Locker Room," *SBNation*, May 7, 2013,

https://www.acmepackingcompany.com/2013/5/7/4307998
/vince-lombardi-packers-acceptance-gay-athletes.

43. Jill Colvin, "DNC, Clinton campaign agree to Steele dossier funding fine," *Associated Press*, March 31, 2022, https://apnews
.com/article/russia-ukraine-2022-midterm-elections-business
-elections-presidential-elections-5468774d18e8c46f81b55e926
0b13e93.

44. Rose Maura Lorre, "50 Vince Lombardi Quotes to Inspire You on Super Bowl Sunday—and Every Day," Parade, February 10, 2024, https://parade.com/1334566/rose-maura-lorre/vince
-lombardi-quotes/.

45. Rose Maura Lorre, "50 Vince Lombardi Quotes to Inspire You on Super Bowl Sunday—and Every Day," Parade, February 10, 2024, https://parade.com/1334566/rose-maura-lorre/vince
-lombardi-quotes/.

46. *The New Oxford Annotated Bible* with Apocrypha